D0783540

HAMLYN
ALL COLOUR
FLOWER
GARDENING

HAMLYN
ALL COLOUR
FLOWER
GARDENING

BCA
LONDON · NEW YORK · SYDNEY · TORONTO

This book has been written by Suzy Powling.
and compiled from material previously published by
Octopus Illustrated Publishing

Art Editor Robin Whitecross Editor Anna Mumford
Picture Research Emily Hedges Production Michele Thomas

Illustrations by Vicky Emptage
Symbols by Coryn Dickman

This edition published 1992 by BCA by arrangement with
Hamlyn which is an imprint of Octopus Illustrated Publishing,
part of Reed International Books Limited,
Michelin House, 81 Fulham Road, London SW3 6RB

© 1992 Reed International Books Limited

All rights reserved. No part of this publication may be reproduced, stored in a retrieval system,
or transmitted, in any form or by any means, electronic, mechanical, photocopying or otherwise,
without the prior written permission of the publisher

A catalogue record for this book is available from
the British Library

CN 3562

Typeset in Sabon

Produced by Mandarin Offset
Printed in Hong Kong

The Publishers would like to thank the following organizations and individuals
for their kind permission to reproduce the photographs in this book.

Special Photography: Mark Williams, 10 top and bottom, 11 top and bottom, 12,

Bernard Alfieri, 37 left; K&G Beckett, 117 right; Pat Brindley, 50 left, 68 left, 79 right ;
Eric Crichton, front cover right, title page left, centre and right, 20, 21, 31 right, 32 left, 35 right, 47 right, 55 right, 65 right,
70 left, 76, 79 left, 81 left, 83 left, 84 right, 92 right, 93 right, 94 left, 95 right, 99 left 111 left;
Brian Furner, 114 left; Garden Picture Library /Derek Fell, 28 left, 54 left, 61, 75 right; Derek Gould, 27 right, 53 left, 64 right, 83 right,
89 right, 113 right; Jerry Harpur, back jacket top centre, 77; Anthony Huxley, 37 right ;
Tania Midgely, 26 right, 30 right, 34 right, 71 right, 81 right, 109 left, 124 left; NHPA/M Savonius, 46 right;
Harry Smith Collection, 25 left, 27 left, 34 left, 49 left, 58 left, 70 right, 82 left, 85 right, 95 left,
96, 97, 104 left, 107 right, 114 right, 123 right; Octopus Picture Library, 14, /Michael Boys, 25 right, 31 left,
36 left and right, 48 right, 60, 68 right, 74 left, 78 left and right, 82 right, 85 left, 92 left,
98 right, 100 right, 103 right, 105 left, 108 right, 115 right, 118, 122 left, 123 left, 125 right, /Jerry Harpur, front jacket left and centre,
back jacket top left and top right, half title, 6, 8, 23 right, 24 left, 30 left, 33 right,
35 left, 38, 39, 40 left and right, 41 left, 42 left and right, 43 right, 44 left, 45 left, 46 left, 49 right, 50 right,
51 left and right, 52 left, 53 right, 54 right, 55 left, 56 left, 57 left and right, 58 right, 59 right, 63 left, 65 left, 66 right, 69 left and right,
71 left, 72 left and right, 73 left and right, 74 right, 80 left, 84 left, 86 right,
87 right, 88 left and right, 89 left, 90 left and right, 91 left and right, 94 right, 99 right, 100 left,
102 left and right, 103 left, 110 left, 112 left and right, 113 left, 115 left, 116 left and right, 117 left, 121 left and right, 124 right,
125 left, 126 right, /Neil Holmes, 33 left, 64 left, 87 left, 98 left, 107 left,
/George Wright, back jacket bottom left and bottom right, 22 left and right, 23 left, 24 right, 26 left, 28 right, 29 left and right,
32 right, 41 right, 43 left, 44 right, 45 right, 47 left, 48 left, 52 right, 56 right, 59 left,
62 left and right, 63 right, 66 left, 67 left and right, 75 left, 80 right, 86 left, 101 left and right, 104 right, 105 right, 106 left and right,
108 left, 110 right, 111 right, 120 left and right, 122 right, 126 left; Photos Horticultural/Michael Warren, 93 left, 109 right ;

CONTENTS

INTRODUCTION

The choice of plants available to the gardener today is bewildering in its breadth and variety. This book aims to make the selection easier by focusing on a selection of beautiful flowering plants – some old favourites, some less well-known – which deserve a place in the modern garden. They have been grouped according to type – annuals, perennials, bulbs, alpines, shrubs and climbers, and trees. Every plant is illustrated and, for quick reference, symbols are given to indicate important factors such as flowering time, degree of hardiness, the plant's dimensions and preferred site.

Accompanying each illustration is a brief description of the plant, advice on successful growing and propagation and details of other varieties, where available, which are particularly recommended. Recognizing the fact that most of us are attracted to flowers by their colour, the plants within each chapters have been grouped by colour wherever possible to give an idea of the marvellous variety of blooms that nature has to offer which, with a little love and care, will ornament your garden throughout many seasons.

IN THE FLOWER GARDEN

Gardening is one of life's most creative activities. Whether a garden extends to several acres or is confined to a few square yards, the gardener brings it to life, deciding what to plant and where, what to move – and sometimes what to discard.

All these decisions are affected by certain factors which must be taken into account in order to achieve success. The most important of these are climate, site and soil. To a large extent you must work with what you are given – human beings have no control over the weather, for example – and it is essential to identify these factors before you can accommodate or improve them.

CLIMATE Climate includes many variables – rainfall, humidity, temperature, wind and intensity of light – which influence the kind of plants that will thrive in the region where you live. The first factor to take into account is whether a particular plant can withstand the lowest temperatures likely to occur. Most of the plants described in this book are hardy in temperate zones, meaning that they need no protection at any point in their life cycle – provided you live in a temperate zone. Some, however, will only thrive against a warm, sunny wall. Half-hardy plants need protection during the winter, such as a cloche or a covering of straw or hessian; tender plants need permanent protection such as that afforded by a greenhouse, but a few can be set outside in the heat of summer.

There are plants with particular likes and dislikes, such as clematis, which likes a cool root run, or camellia, which should not be placed where early morning sun after frost might damage young growth. To help a plant give of its best, it is important to observe these individual requirements. Plant some *Alchemilla mollis* where it will cast shade over the roots of a clematis, and do not site your camellia on a wall which gets the morning sun.

RAINFALL Excessive rainfall causes a problem in gardens where drainage is poor, though this can sometimes be corrected. Even so it may make life difficult for plants like alpines and others that like a sunny, dry bank. Some flowers are badly damaged by rain – white roses, for example – and wind after rain can be devastating. Lack of rain is a more general problem. In areas where rainfall is low, it makes sense to concentrate on plants that can cope with drought *(see page 18)* and to use moisture-retentive mulches of peat, leaf-mould, spent hops, garden compost, well-rotted manure or pulverized bark on plants that need it – particularly shrubs, roses, trees, dahlias and sweet peas.

SUN AND SHADE There are many splendid plants that will only give of their best if they receive a full day's sunshine. However, many more will be sustained by just a few hours every day, and most gardens, however ill-favoured they seem, will enjoy some sunshine for at least part of the day. The blessing is that there are so many desirable plants which prefer shade or semi-shade *(see page 18)*. Take note of the source of the shade and plan accordingly: a large tree will not only cast a correspondingly large shadow, but take all the nutrients from the soil around it, so that no other plants can thrive. A shaded wall will be cool but need not be bare: clematis, jasmine, honeysuckles and some roses will do well in such a situation *(see page 18)*.

WINDS Occasional fierce winds are a hazard most gardeners try to become philosophical about. On sites where strong winds are a more regular feature, it makes sense to erect barriers in the form of quick-growing dense hedges or fences that can be clothed with climbers – both are better than brick walls, which can trap pockets of frost. Flowering shrubs suitable for hedging include deutzia, forsythia, fuchsia, lavender, pyracantha, roses, santolina, lilac and viburnum.

SANDY SOIL

The particles of sandy soil are relatively large so that water drains away quickly, taking valuable nutrients with it. In periods of drought, the soil tends to dry out. The advantage of open-textured soil is a good air supply to plants' roots, encouraging deep development. Sandy soils are light, easy to work and warm up quickly. The best way to improve fertility on such soils is to incorporate quantities of organic manures of any type. Keep well-watered in dry weather.

CLAY SOIL

Generally cold and wet, clay soils do not admit much air to the root systems of plants, inhibiting the development and as a result reducing the amount of top growth. Because they are slow to warm up, clay soils are inhospitable to early-flowering varieties. Clay soils can be improved, and again the means of doing so is plenty of organic matter Clay soils also benefit from so-called 'green manures' (*see page 11*). It is advisable to apply lime to break down the soil's close structure and improve drainage. Apply ground limestone at 100g/m ^{2} (4oz per sq yd) every other year in the autumn. Clay soils retain their fertilizer content well, and plants rarely suffer from drought. Roses and many perennials like a well-maintained clay soil.

UNDERSTANDING THE SOIL

Plants derive the nourishment they need in order to thrive from the soil. Keeping the soil in good condition is a gardener's most important task. The first step is to identify the type of soil in your garden – bearing in mind that a large plot may contain more than one type. The ideal soil is known as loam: it is dark, has a crumbly texture, drains well but retains enough moisture to supply plants' need for water. It has a high content of decaying organic matter, sustaining plenty of earthworms and beneficial insects and contributing to fertility. Loamy soils warm up relatively quickly, making it easier to succeed with early-flowering varieties. The only requirements for keeping loam in good condition are generous applications of well-rotted compost or other organic matter (*see page 11*). 'Green manures' (quick-growing crops such as mustard or red clover that are dug back into the soil while still young and green) are also effective for improving poor soils and maintaining good loam. Like many other ideals, loam is a rarity. Some soils may approach it, but in practice most approximate to one of the types illustrated on pages 10 and 11.

ACID OR ALKALINE? Soil acidity is determined by the amount of lime in the soil. A very chalky or limy soil is said to be alkaline; one which contains little lime is said to be acid. Acidity is expressed on a measure known as the pH scale. Handy, easy-to-use kits are available to test the soil. Mix a small quantity of soil with the indicator fluid in the kit and compare the colour with those on the chart supplied. A neutral soil (green) will have a pH reading of 7. Any reading higher than this (blue) indicates an increase in alkalinity; a much lower reading (red) indicates high acidity. Loamy soils are generally slightly acid with a pH reading of 6.5. This is the level preferred by most plants (including vegetables). Sandy soils are usually acid, though not excessively so. Clay soils need lime. Chalky soils obviously are not, even if, as is sometimes the case, the top few centimetres are slightly acid: for a long period, enough limestone will be brought to the surface by cultivation to balance this out. Peaty soils are notably acid and require heavy dressings of lime every three years. Lime should be applied to the soil surface, preferably

CHALKY SOIL

Soils on chalk are characteristically pale, light in texture and quick-draining. Chalk, or limestone, is an active chemical which combines with certain elements in the soil and renders them unavailable to plants. Deprived of essential trace elements such as iron, manganese, boron or zinc, some plants suffer from serious deficiency diseases and cannot survive. Plants which hate lime include rhododendrons, azaleas, most heaths and heathers and camellies. Happily, the list of lime-tolerant plants (*see page 18*) includes many beautiful species. Again, improvement is down to plenty of organic matter to prevent the soil becoming impoverished.

PEATY SOILS

Dark brown in colour and low in nutrients, peat contains a plant material which because of poor drainage has not completely decomposed. It is essential to improve drainage, by structural means if necessary (laying drains 12-18in/45-67cm below the surface), by regular cultivation (digging in plenty of organic matter) and by applying limestone except in those areas where you might grow plants such as rhododendrons, azaleas or heathers, which like the acidity of peat.

in the autumn or early spring. Delay the use of any artificial fertilizer for eight weeks thereafter. Little can be done to affect alkalinity, and such soils cannot support acid-loving plants like rhododendrons.

IMPROVING THE SOIL All soils benefit from the incorporation of organic matter, not only to replace nutrients used up by plants and to maintain fertility, but also to improve the soil structure. There are a number of forms of organic matter which can be used for this purpose. The best type of animal manure is wheat-straw based horse manure, but it is too strong to be used fresh. Let it rot down completely first – this will take 3-6 months. Well-rotted manure is usually spread on top of the soil in the autumn and dug in in the winter, and should be incorporated into the planting hole when planting roses and trees.

Compost is formed from rotted vegetable matter such as lawn mowings and kitchen waste – for example, potato peelings and crushed eggshells. A compost heap is an excellent source of bulky organic material. Purpose-built compost bins are useful for small gardens. Start with a 15cm/6in layer of coarse material like straw to allow air to circulate while keeping the temperature up, and add the waste material in batches, an 20cm/8in layer at a time to prevent it compacting down. Water lightly if it looks like drying out. Add small quantities of farmyard manure if available and dust occasionally with ground limestone to speed up decomposition. In summer this process takes about three months, in winter at least twice as long.

Leaf-mould is one of the easiest composts to make. It is a very slow procedure but produces one of the best surface mulches and is a useful ingredient for potting composts. It takes two years for a heap of leaves to rot down to a good crumbly consistency. If you have the space and the leaves – which are, after all, completely free – make a simple frame in a dry shady spot from four posts pushed into the ground with wire netting stretched around them. Peat is useful on very light soils, efficiently retaining water in dry weather, and is an excellent mulch for roses. But peat is a non-renewable natural resource, and some gardeners are reluctant to use it. Other useful organic substances are spent hops, seaweed, wood ash in small quantities and spent mushroom compost.

Within the image, handwritten annotations read:
Delphiniums up to 3 feet.
lupins - 3 feet average
Nigella (love in the mist) - 2 feet
Dianthus approx 2ft
Geranium endressii 1 foot
lobelia up to 4 in.
Lavender
1 2 3 4 5 feet

PLANNING YOUR GARDEN

Strategies for garden design differ according to whether you are starting with a virgin plot or working with some established features. There are advantages and shortcomings to both situations.

THE FIRST STEP With a virgin plot, although getting the soil into shape is likely to be a major task, in terms of design you can let your imagination have free rein. In the case of an established garden, you will know what kinds of plants are likely to thrive, and are certain to have inherited at least one feature, perhaps a mature tree or fine hedge, which provides a focal point or good background and gives an air of permanence.

THE PLAN Before drawing up a plan, list all the practical functions your garden must fulfil, such as a play area for children, an area for drying washing or a plot of herbs near the house. You will need somewhere to keep garden tools, and can site a shed for storage where it will be inconspicuous, yet not using up a favourable spot better suited to a deserving shrub. Make a plan on paper by all means, but do not let arm-chair planning take over from walking around the garden at different times of day, noting how the light falls and how the garden looks from different angles. Remember, too, to take into account what you can see, or would rather not see, in your neighbours' gardens and beyond.

If you do not know where to start, have a look at as many other gardens as you can. Literally hundreds of them, great and small, are open to the public and are unquestionably the best source of ideas.

FORMAL DESIGNS Garden designs are basically formal or informal. A large formal garden is difficult and costly to maintain, but a formal design can succeed very well in small gardens, particularly in town, and need not be demanding once laid out, especially if paving is used rather than lawns and planting is confined to shrubs, low-maintenance perennials and bulbs. Such designs are enhanced by a limited colour palette, giving a sense of peace and order. Silver, green and white is a justifiably popular combination. It associates well with paving and statuary and allows for focus on the shape of individual plants. Concentrating on any single flower colour will have the same effect, though soft blues and yellows tend to be more successful than vivid pinks, reds or orange.

In formal gardens straight lines predominate, balanced with carefully controlled curves, and each element must be in harmony with the rest. Plants with handsome foliage are particularly appropriate here, especially if they can be grouped around a small pool. Some plants with attractive foliage described in this book are the shrubs potentilla, mahonia, santolina, pieris, camellia and species clematis, with enkianthus and fothergilla for autumn colour, and the perennials alchemilla, euphorbia, pulmonaria and bergenia. Dwarf tulips and narcissi are bulbs worth considering.

INFORMAL DESIGNS Restraint and simplicity are essential to garden design, even if the end result is informal and apparently random, as in the ever-popular cottage garden. In such designs the rounded lines of generously planted bushy specimens, twining climbers and arching stems are held in check by straight-line boundaries of paved paths and low hedges. The paths will be of soft-coloured materials like brick or York stone, laid so that thyme, for example, can take hold between the cracks. Hedges might be lavender or santolina. Against a permanent backdrop of shrubs and climbers such as rambling roses, fragrant honeysuckle and scrambling *Clematis montana*, cottage gardens are populated by a wide range of perennials and annuals.

The selection of suitable plants reflects principles relevant to any mixed planting for beds and borders. There must be plants that give height situated at the rear, in this case delphiniums, lupins or lilies perhaps. Colours will be varied, with clumps of the eye-catching poppies and marigolds judiciously set among dense-leaved plants as a green foil.

Getting the palette right – for blues and pinks will inevitably be equally well represented by the likes of love-in-a-mist, forget-me-nots, crane's-bills and cornflowers – takes considerable skill and a certain amount of trial and error. It is comforting to remember that, whatever the effect they are striving for, many gardeners eventually discard up to half their original choice of plants before they feel they have it right. Patience is probably the good gardener's most valuable asset.

A WILD AREA Many people now like to incorporate a 'wild' area in their garden if they have the space. This will not in fact be an area left to nature – that is the opposite of a garden, after all – but one that appears to be so. In the open it might well include bulbs such as *Narcissus cyclamineus* which can be planted in sweeps to fend for themselves. This type of planting is called naturalizing, and typically uses plants like daffodils and crocuses whose foliage is grass-like. Under trees, *Cyclamen neapolitanum*, lily-of-the-valley and snowdrops do well. The area between 'wild' and cultivated garden might well be marked by a strip of long grass, bordering the lawn.

LAWNS Making and caring for lawns is beyond the scope of this book, but in terms of design it is worth pointing out that a swathe of grass – as well kept as you can manage – is the most obvious evergreen element you can include. It is a neutral space against which all other plants are set, restful to the eye and a perfect backdrop to the plants displayed in the border.

GARDEN TASKS

Gardens are places for relaxation and contemplation, it is true; nevertheless there are a number of jobs which need regular attention.

WEEDING Weeds are unsightly and compete with plants for nourishment from the soil. Perennial weeds should be resolutely dug out and burned and will disappear within 2-3 years. Annual weeds should be removed as soon as seen, never let them get to the flowering stage. Use ground cover plants and mulches to smother weeds.

WATERING Seedlings which have just been planted out and container-grown perennials and shrubs should be watered in and kept lightly and frequently watered until established. In summer, an occasional good watering at a cool time of day is ideal. To conserve moisture, apply mulches and protect plants from wind, which dries out the surface

DIGGING If you are starting a garden from scratch in a plot attached to a new house, revitalizing an existing garden or setting out a new border, digging will be essential to clear the ground of rubble and unwanted vegetation, simultaneously aerating the soil.

FEEDING All plants need nitrogen, phosphate and potash plus some trace elements such as iron and zinc to grow. Nitrogen is important for leaf growth, phosphate for root development and potash for flowers. Organic fertilizers contain varying amounts of these substances, which they release gradually into the soil. Chemical fertilizers may contain a balance of all three or one may predominate. Organic gardeners are anti chemical fertilizers because they believe that they make plants prone to pests and diseases without feeding the soil in the long term. On the credit side, chemical fertilizers are easy to use and produce quick results. A compound fertilizer is best, applied as a light top dressing at the rate of 15g/m^2 (½ oz per sq yd). Spread the fertilizer evenly by hand, three or four times during the season.

PROPAGATION

Raising your own plants is a tremendously satisfying process, and can provide new material for very little expense. Different methods are suitable for different types of plants.

CUTTINGS Cuttings may be taken from various parts of a plant. For the plants in this book stem cuttings are most generally used. They are usually rooted in a growing medium of equal parts (by volume) peat

This well planned planting shows skilful handling of plant colour, height and form. Toning shades of green provide the backdrop to strong punctuations of colour.

SOFT CUTTINGS

These are immature non-flowering shoot tips. Many perennials and sub-shrubs are increased in this way, for example pelargoniums. Make a sharp cut just below a node and remove the bottom pair of leaves before placing the cutting in the rooting medium. Sometimes it is best to take a cutting with a heel, as described below. Soft cuttings take 10-30 days to take root.

SEMI-RIPE CUTTINGS

These are firmer than soft cuttings. They are usually taken in summer and do not need added heat; a cold frame is the best environment. Shrubs and heathers are increased in this way. Take a cutting from a healthy side shoot, if necessary with a heel, a small piece of older wood, attached. Cleanly cut off the soft tip and remove the lowest pair of leaves before inserting in the rooting medium. Keep the frame closed and spray on warm days to keep it moist. The cuttings should be ready for planting out in nursery rows the following spring. Any that have not rooted should be discarded.

Hardwood Cuttings

These are suitable for trees, shrubs and roses. Take a cutting between 15 and 37cm/6 and 15in long (only 25cm/10in for roses), with a heel if necessary (rose cuttings need a heel). Remove all but the top three pairs of leaves. If there is an unripened shoot at the tip, cut back to a suitable bud. Take out a V-shaped trench 25cm/10in deep in good, weed-free soil and place a shallow layer of sand at the bottom to assist drainage. Insert the cuttings to half to two-thirds their length against the vertical side of the trench and push the soil back from the other side. Plant very firmly. Leave for at least a year, or until the rooted cuttings have increased to a healthy size, before transferring to the permanent positions.

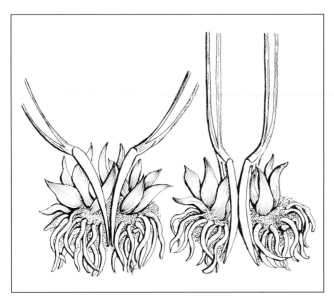

Division

Most perennials are increased by division, and some need dividing from time to time if they become overcrowded. Lift the plant when dormant – between autumn and spring. Separate the sections by hand, trowel or two forks (*above*) in the case of larger plants. Discard the central, woody sections and replant the outer parts. Tough crowns such as lupins should be washed free of soil and the sections cut up with a sharp knife. Make sure each part has roots and buds before replanting.

and sand, though in certain cases other mixtures have been recommended. In order for a cutting to take root it needs light, warmth and moisture. The size of the cuttings and the best time of year to take them are given in the individual entries. Most cuttings of hardy plants taken in summer will root readily in a cold frame without heat. Cuttings taken from growing plants in cold seasons require some heat. An electrically heated propagator is a good way of providing this.

Hardwood cuttings are used for trees, shrubs, old roses, species roses and miniature roses and are taken between autumn and spring when the plant is dormant. Semi-ripe cuttings are used for increasing shrubs and heathers; and soft cuttings are used to propagate many perennials and sub-shrubs, like pelargoniums.

RAISING PLANTS FROM SEED Most plants can be raised from seed, though some take literally years to germinate. In practice you will find it useful to raise most of your annuals in this way. Seeds of hardy annuals may be sown outside in spring in a well-prepared bed. Water the soil the day before. Mark out shallow drills with the side of a hoe, sow the seed thinly along the row and cover lightly with soil. Alternatively, scatter seed on the ground and rake it in. Firm the soil with the flat side of the rake. Water well, with a fine rose the day after sowing and again a week later.

Half-hardy annuals can be raised from seed sown indoors from spring onwards. Fill a seed tray with moist seed compost and press down evenly and firmly. Place the seeds on top, evenly spaced. Cover with 5mm/¼in of sifted compost and water in gently until the compost is thoroughly wet. Cover with a sheet of glass or polythene and place in a heated frame or propagator; or cover with a plastic bag and place in a warm dark place, such as an airing cupboard. Check daily for moisture on the inside of the bag, which should be flicked off. As soon as the seed leaves appear, remove the cover and move to a protected position in the light.

THINNING Thin the seedlings out when they have two or three true leaves (not the tiny seed leaves that appear after germination has taken place). Take care not to disturb the seedlings left behind (a wooden ice lollipop stick makes an efficient 'trowel') Retain only the strongest and discard the weak ones.

LAYERING

Some plants layer themselves naturally and a number of other plants can be persuaded to reproduce themselves in this way. It works well for many shrubs and is often used for dianthus. Autumn is the best time. Prepare the soil by digging it over and adding peat if it is on the light side. Select a healthy one-year-old non-flowering branch. Remove a portion of leaves, not from the tip itself but the next 30cm/12in section of stem. Make a shallow sloping cut in the underside of the branch. Bend it at the cut, without breaking the stem and place the cut portion on the ground. Peg it in place, with the growing tip pointing upwards. Cover the cut with compost and water in. Healthy roots should have developed from the cut within a year. At this point the branch can be severed from its parent and set in its permanent position.

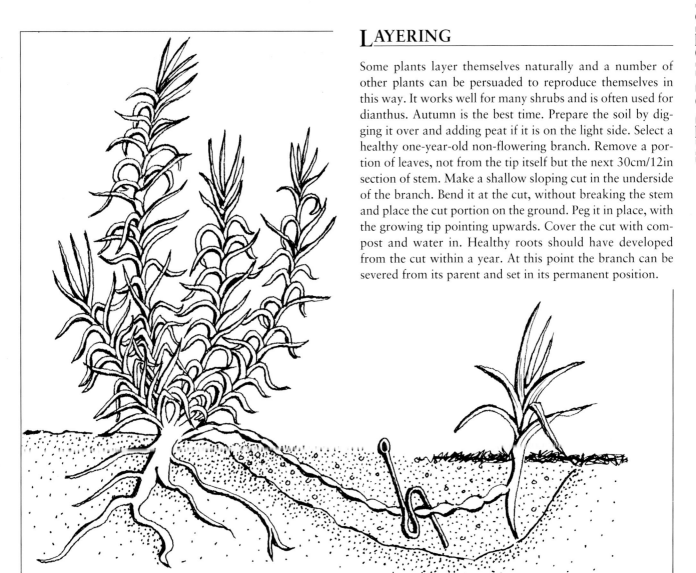

PRICKING OUT When the true leaves appear the seedlings can be pricked off into trays or 7.5cm/3in pots of potting compost. Prepare planting holes with a pencil, spacing them 4cm/½in apart. Carefully remove a small clump of seedlings with a plastic plant tag or similar tool, holding them by the leaves, never the roots. Separate them gently and lower them one by one into the planting holes. Use a pencil to firm the compost around each one. Water in using a fine rose watering can. Place the tray in a cold frame or on a windowsill away from direct sunlight for two to three days, then move into a sunlit position. The compost should be kept moist. Harden off the seedlings gradually by exposing them to increasing amounts of fresh air during the day. When they are hardened off they may be planted in their permanent positions. Make sure the soil is moist when planting and take care not to damage the root system when transferring the young plants from the trays or pots to the flowerbed.

OFFSETS

These are small bulbils or cormlets naturally formed at the side of a parent bulb. They are easy to detach from the parent when lifting for storage and are best planted in a nursery bed for 2 years until they reach flowering size.

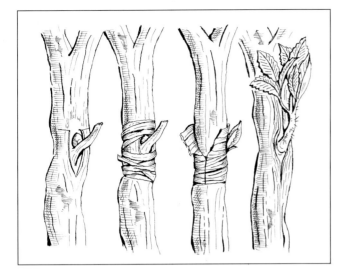

BUDDING

A relatively complex form of propagation used for certain types of roses and some ornamental trees. Basically it involves taking a bud from the plant you wish to increase and inserting it in a T-shaped cut on suitable rootstock. The bud must fit the cut very closely and be tightly bound with raffia. When it has 'taken', the rootstock is cut down to just above the bud. Any shoots appearing from the rootstock itself must be removed, or they will take over the plant.

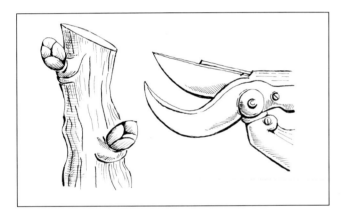

PRUNING

A certain mystique is attached to pruning, but it is based on simple enough principles. Many shrubs must have some branches or shoots periodically removed in order to keep their shape and go on producing good flowers. A tangled mass of stems is not only unsightly but prevents healthy air circulation, encouraging pests and diseases. Use good sharp secateurs to make sure all pruning cuts are clean. Remove branches or stems close to an outward-facing bud with a cut sloping away from it as shown above. Pruning to remove damaged wood can be done at any time. Many gardeners go over shrubs in spring for this purpose to clear up the devastation of winter, simultaneously removing weak branches and shortening by half any that are unsightly. Shrubs that flower on the previous season's wood, such as deutzia, *Spiraea x arguta* and *Mahonia aquifolium* (as ground cover) are pruned immediately after flowering. Cut back hard to a new shoot. Shrubs that flower on new shoots such as deciduous ceanothus, fuchsia, santolina and most spiraeas may be pruned in early spring to encourage healthy, compact plants . Cut the previous year's shoots to 2 or 3 buds from their base.

PLANT FINDER

DROUGHT-RESISTANT PLANTS

ANNUALS *Centaurea, Mesembryanthemum, Salvia, Zinnia*
PERENNIALS *Catananche, Helichrysum, Hemerocallis, Oenothera*
ALPINES *Aethionema, Iberis, Juniperus, Santolina, Saponaria, Sedum, Thymus*
BULBS *Crocus chrysanthus, Gladiolus, Iris danfordiae, Narcissus cyclamineus, Scilla peruviana*
SHRUBS *Cytisus, Hibiscus, Lavandula*

PLANTS FOR SHADE

ANNUALS *Asperula*
PERENNIALS *Aquilegia, Bergenia, Convallaria, Fothergilla, Helleborus, Polyanthus, Pulmonaria, Tiarella, Viola*
BULBS *Cyclamen, Eranthis, Galanthus*
SHRUBS *Mahonia, Rhododendron*
CLIMBERS *Clematis, Jasminum, Lonicera, Wistaria, Pyracantha,* roses including *'Danse du Feu', 'Caroline Testout', 'Parkdirektor Riggers'* and *'Paul's Lemon Pillar'*

LIME-TOLERANT PLANTS

ALPINES *Erodium, Helianthemum*
SHRUBS *Deutzia, Forsythia, Fuchsia, Philadelphus, Rosa species, Spiraea, Syringa, Viburnum*
CLIMBERS *Clematis, Lonicera*

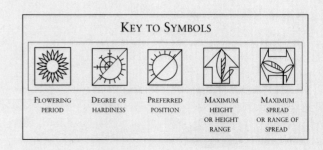

KEY TO SYMBOLS

| FLOWERING PERIOD | DEGREE OF HARDINESS | PREFERRED POSITION | MAXIMUM HEIGHT OR HEIGHT RANGE | MAXIMUM SPREAD OR RANGE OF SPREAD |

PESTS AND DISEASES

PESTS

PROBLEM	DAMAGE CAUSED	REMEDY
Aphids (greenfly, blackfly)	Sap sucked; honeydew emitted, virus diseases spread	Spray with pirimicarb
Capsid bug	Leaves tattered or with tiny holes	Spray with systemic insecticide
Caterpillar	Leaves, stems, flowers eaten	Spray with permethrin or trichlorphon
Earwig	Flowers, shoot-tips, young leaves eaten	Trap with straw-filled inverted flowerpots on canes among plants; kill with malathion or HCH
Eelworm	Plants weakened, leaves and stems distorted	Destroy infected plants, do not grow again on same site
Froghopper	Sap sucked under cuckoospit	Spray with fenitrothion
Leaf miner	Pale tunnels in leaves	Remove infested leaves; spray with pirimphos-methyl
Lily beetle	Leaves eaten	Spray with pirimphos-methyl
Mealy bug	Sap sucked, virus diseases spread by small insect enclosed in white 'wool'	Spray with malathion
Narcissus fly	No flowers; weak, grassy leaves; maggots in bulbs	Destroy infested (soft) bulbs
Red-spider mite	Sap sucked; foliage desiccated; fine webs spun	Spray with fenitrothion or malathion
Rhododendron bug	Leaves mottled, yellow above and brown below	Spray leaf undersides with pirimphos-methyl
Sawfly	Leaves eaten or rolled under	Spray in late spring with pirimphos-methyl
Scale insects	Sap sucked, virus diseases spread by small, limpet-like insects	Spray with malathion
Slugs and snails	Young plant leaves eaten	Scatter methiocarb thinly among plants
Tarsonemid mite	Stems, flowers distorted and scarred; leaves, stems spoon-like	Dig up and burn affected plants; do not grow again on the site
Thrips	White speckles, then grey patches on leaves, flowers	Spray with fenitrothion
Vine weevil	Lower leaves holed and notched; grubs on roots, plants wilt	Dust lower leaves and soil with HCH
Whitefly	Sap sucked; virus diseases spread	Spray with permethrin

DISEASES

Anthracnose of willow	Small brown canker on stems; die back of stem tips; blotched leaves fall	Spray with thiophanate-methyl
Azalea gall	Hard green reddish or whitish swellings on leaves and buds	Cut out and burn infected stems; spray with copper fungicide
Bacterial canker	Leaves full of holes; stem cankers with oozing gum; general weakening	Cut out infected wood; spray with benomyl
Blackspot	Rose leaves develop black spots, fall early	Rake up and burn all leaves at end of season; spray with bupirimate and triforine
Botrytis (Grey mould)	Parts of plants rot, become covered in grey fur	Remove and burn infected parts; spray with benomyl
Bud blast	Rhododendron buds turn brown, develop black pinhead spore capsules and fail to open	Cut off infected buds; spray with fenitrothion to control leafhoppers that spread the disease
Canker	Rough brown sunken areas on stems	Cut out and burn; spray with thiophanate-methyl
Chlorosis	Leaves yellowed; growth stunted on alkaline soils	Grow plants on acid soils. Water with iron sequestrene; feed well
Clematis wilt	Collapse of mature shoots, usually on young plants	Cut back to ground level; water with benomyl
Coral spot	Raised orange pustules on woody stems	Cut out infected wood and burn; paint wounds with sealant
Die-back	Woody stems die at tips	Cut out infected wood back to healthy tissue
Fireblight	Shoots, flowers look burned, turn brown and wilt	Cut out infected stems back to healthy tissue; paint wounds with sealant
Fusarium wilt	Lower leaves and stem bases turn brown and rot	Destroy infected plants; do not grow species again on the same ground.
Honey fungus	Stems die back (or plants even die) for no visible reason. Fungal 'bootlaces' found in soil; honey-coloured toadstools on site	Dig up and burn infected plants; dig up all tree stumps. Water soil with fungicide
Leaf spot	Dark blotches on leaves	Spray with copper fungicide in spring. Prevent by growing on good soil
Lilac blight	Black spots on leaves; shoots wither	Cut out infected wood; spray with bordeaux mixture
Mildew	White powder or downy deposit on leaves and stems	Cut out badly infected growth; spray with benomyl
Peony wilt	Leaf bases of herbaceous peonies turn brown and rot	Destroy infected buds or plants. Prevent by spraying with dichlofluanid
Petal blight	Petals covered by translucent spots, especially in wet weather	Remove and destroy infected blooms
Root rot	Roots turn brown and rot, killing plant	Destroy infected plants
Rust	Yellow spots on upper leaf surfaces, orange pustules below	Destroy infected plants; spray others with mancozeb. Prevent by growing resistant strains
Scab	Reddish-brown spots on leaves; black spots on corms	Dip corms in calomel dust
Sclerotinia	White fungal growth coats stems, makes plant collapse. Black resting bodies overwinter in soil	Destroy infected plants. Do not grow dahlias on site
Virus diseases	Leaves distorted, marbled, yellowed; plant often stunted	Dig up and burn; control insect disease-carriers

ANNUALS

Annuals are plants that complete their life cycle in one season, while biennials need two seasons, producing leaves in the first year, flowers and seeds in the second.

Sometimes the distinctions between types are affected by climate; for example, in cooler zones the perennial antirrhinum is grown as an annual. Sometimes annuals perpetuate themselves, scattering seed that readily germinates where it falls. Love-in-a-mist *(Nigella damascena)* is an annual that provides you with flowers year after year in this way.

Annuals have a multitude of roles to play in the garden. They are particularly valuable when you are starting from scratch and are confronted with bare patches of earth, with a few young shrubs and perennials as yet too small to have much effect. Seeds of annuals sown in the spring will provide a colourful display for the whole of those first summers while more permanent plants are becoming established. This also gives you an opportunity to play with ideas about colours and arrangements of colours within particular beds: does a palette of soft blues and pinks look pleasing near the house? Will a dull corner be brought to life with gleaming reds and yellows? Experiments with annuals help you make decisions that have longer-term effects on the overall appearance of your plot.

Even when the basic framework of the garden, provided by trees, shrubs and perennials, is beginning to take shape, most gardeners like to introduce a fresh note of colour into the summer garden by using annuals. The fun lies in ringing the changes and trying out different colour combinations and new varieties of plants each year. Both house and garden benefit from this versatility, as many annuals last well as cut flowers. Serious flower arrangers who need a steady supply of plant material may consider devoting a patch of the vegetable garden to their favourites so that they do not have to deplete the garden's display.

Annuals are relatively time-consuming, calling for regular watering, staking in some cases, weeding and dead-heading. The amount of space you allocate them will therefore depend to some extent on the amount of time you have available to devote to them. Another consideration is cost: if you do not raise your own plants from seed, buying them as bedding plants from a garden centre or nursery can prove expensive.

SITING Choose and site carefully to make the most of your purchases, planting them in tight groups to make an impact rather than setting them too far apart just to fill a space. When designing a bed of annuals, the usual common-sense rules apply about placing tall-growing specimens such as larkspur *(Delphinium ajacis)*, cosmos and lavatera at the back, with clumps of medium height in the centre and dwarfs for edging at the front. Low, spreading plants will help to smother weeds, too. Try to strike a balance between different shapes, including some straight-stemmed showy speci-

This beautiful display of Convolvulus tricolor *(left),* Lychnis coronaria *(front) and* Cosmos *(back) fills the herbacous border with colour during the summer.*

mens like rudbeckias and some that provide a cloud of delicate colour like gypsophila. Contrast the ragged heads of cornflowers *(Centaurea* species) with daisy-like chrysanthemums and frilly sweet peas.

CONTAINERS Annuals come into their own in the planting up of containers. The bleakest spot can be completely transformed by pots, tubs, window-boxes and hanging baskets spilling over with summer flowers. As well as pelargoniums and impatiens (*see Perennials*), petunias, marigolds, lobelia and lobularia do well in containers. For successful results it is important to remember that all containers dry out quickly and need regular watering. Larger containers with correspondingly greater amounts of compost retain moisture longer. Wind dries out the compost as quickly as the heat of the sun.

HANGING BASKETS Hanging baskets are an ingenious way of displaying summer-flowering plants and have become very popular. Wire baskets permit you to trail flowerstems through the mesh, but are slightly tricky to plant up. Balance them on a heavy bucket while you work. Line the basket with a small amount of moss which has been soaked in water and wrung out. Cover with a layer of potting compost. Set plants around the edge, carefully pushing the root balls between the wires. Cover with compost and another batch of plants. Continue in this way until the basket is full. Solid plastic containers with a water reservoir incorporated have a flat base which makes planting and maintenance easier.

Annuals grown in containers need a good peat-based compost with a shallow layer of drainage material at the bottom. Soak the compost thoroughly several hours before planting up and do not let it dry out at any time. Within 2-3 weeks the plants will require supplementary feeding, preferably in the form of liquid fertilizer. Dead-head regularly to encourage the flowering.

COSMOS

| summer/autumn | half hardy | full sun | 45cm-1.2m/18in-4ft | 60cm/24in |

Native to South America, these daisy-like flowers bring vivid colour to borders or containers well into the autumn. Varieties are available in shades of yellow and pink.

PROPAGATION Sow seeds in early spring under protection and with gentle heat. Prick out the seedlings into boxes as soon as they are large enough to handle and harden off before planting out 4-5 weeks after sowing.

GROWING Cosmos like a light soil that is not too rich, and do best in warm, dry weather. The delicate stems need the support of stakes. Dead-head the flowers regularly.

VARIETIES *C. sulphureus*: 'Bright Lights' (*above*) bears small double flowers in yellow, orange and scarlet; 'Sunny Gold' is a dwarf strain with small golden flowers. *C. bipinnatus*: all varieties have fern-like leaves, with flowers of white or deep pink up to 12.5cm/5in across, and reach 1.2m/4ft in height. Choose from 'Candy Stripe', 'Gloria' and 'Sensation Mixed'.

POSSIBLE PROBLEMS Generally trouble-free.

RUDBECKIA

| summer/autumn | hardy | full sun | 30-60cm/12-24in | 45cm /18in |

Rudbeckia hirta, the original Black-eyed Susan, is treated as an annual, though strictly it is a perennial like its relatives *R. laciniata* (the coneflower) and *R. nitida*. Its bright yellow or orange flowers with contrasting dark centres are eye-catching candidates for the border and make good cut flowers.

PROPAGATION Sow seed in early spring in trays in a cold frame or greenhouse. Prick out the seedlings when large enough to handle and plant into the flowering site.

GROWING Annual rudbeckias like a dry, free-draining soil, unlike the perennials which prefer heavy, moisture-retentive loam. They tolerate dappled shade but prefer a sunny position. In the open, support the plants with stakes.

VARIETIES 'Marmalade' bears orange flowers up to 7.5 cm/3in across; 'Rustic Dwarfs' (*above*) are of equal size in shades of orange and bronze.

POSSIBLE PROBLEMS Generally trouble-free.

▦ CUT FLOWER TIP

The height and size of these flowers makes for a striking flower arrangement, but make sure the vase is tall enough, as the stems are fragile and need support.

▦ PLANTING TIP

These flowers are perfect for planting close to the house, where they will contrast effectively with brick walls or evergreen edging such as privet or box. The bright daisy-like blooms appear in late summer, just when the main display of summer-flowering border shrubs begin to dwindle.

TAGETES

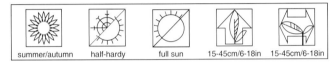

summer/autumn	half-hardy	full sun	15-45cm/6-18in	15-45cm/6-18in

Tagetes patula, the French marigold, is in fact a native of Mexico. Various strains produce flowers of yellow and orange, sometimes blotched with crimson or bronze, some with double flowers. Very long-lived, they add a bright note to the border and make good cut flowers.

PROPAGATION Sow seeds under protection in early spring and prick the seedlings out into boxes when they are large enough to handle. Harden off before planting out in late spring. Pinch out any premature flowerbuds. Seeds may be sown directly into the flowering site in late spring.

GROWING Marigolds are not fussy about soil, but like a sunny, open site. Dead-head regularly to encourage continued flowering. Discard at the end of the season.

VARIETIES Of the many good named varieties, try 'Naughty Marietta', yellow, blotched maroon; 'Monarch Mixed', compact double flowers ranging in colour from yellow to deep mahogany; 'Queen Sophia' syn. 'Scarlet Sophia', double flowers, russet-red laced with gold. *T. patula* is crossed with *T. erecta* to give Afro-French hybrids such as 'Suzie Wong' which are compact and early flowering.

POSSIBLE PROBLEMS Damp conditions cause grey mould.

GAZANIA

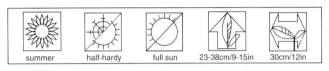

summer	half-hardy	full sun	23-38cm/9-15in	30cm/12in

Only in the very mildest areas can gazanias, natives of South Africa, be grown as perennials; elsewhere they are treated as annuals. The brilliant daisy-like flowers of cream, yellow, orange, crimson or mauve will only open in direct sunlight. The narrow leaves are grey on the underside.

PROPAGATION Sow seeds in very early spring in gentle heat. Prick seedlings into pots when they are large enough to handle. Harden off and plant out in early summer when all danger of frost is past. Tip cuttings may be taken in summer and overwintered in the greenhouse before planting out the following year.

GROWING Gazanias must have full sun; they like well-drained soil, and do well in coastal gardens.

VARIETIES Choose from named hybrids such as 'Chansonette' (*above*), lemon, apricot, orange, carmine red; 'Sundance', large blooms, wide range of colours including cream; 'Mini Star', compact strain, yellow, gold, bronze, red.

POSSIBLE PROBLEMS Damp weather may cause grey mould.

▌ ORGANIC TIP

Ideal for companion planting near roses, or vegetables such as tomatoes, as they attract hover-flies whose larvae eat aphids by the thousand. The hover-fly has a short feeding tube, and so an open-structured flower like tagetes, whose pollen is easily accessible, is an ideal food source.

▌ PROPAGATION TIP

Take cuttings of basal side shoots in mid to late summer. Dip base in hormone rooting compound and plant in sandy soil in pots. Overwinter in greenhouse.

23

GYPSOPHILA

summer	hardy	full sun	30-45cm/12-18in	30-45cm/12-18in

Commonly known as baby's breath or chalk plant, *Gypsophila elegans* is covered with masses of tiny white or pink flowers throughout the summer. It makes a cloudy haze in the border and is indispensable in flower arrangements.

PROPAGATION Sow seeds in the flowering site in early spring or late summer. When the seedlings reach 10-15cm/4-6in, provide twiggy sticks or thin brushwood as supports.

GROWING Gypsophilas need very well-drained soil, preferably alkaline; dress acid soils lightly with lime. Cutting down the stems after flowering may induce a second flush of flowers in late autumn.

VARIETIES 'Alba Grandiflora', 'Covent Garden', white flowers; 'Rosea', vivid pink.

POSSIBLE PROBLEMS Generally trouble-free.

NEMESIA

summer	half-hardy	full sun	30-45cm/12-18in	15-20cm/6-8in

The velvety flowers of nemesia are like a smaller version of antirrhinums, and come in an equally dazzling range of colours suitable for the summer border. The bushy plants bear their flowers in clusters above pointed, light green leaves.

PROPAGATION Sow seed in early spring under protection and with gentle heat. Prick the seedlings out into boxes when they are large enough to handle. Harden off before setting plants into their flowering positions in late spring.

GROWING Nemesias are cheerful, showy plants, but the blooms fade quickly if in very hot sun. Set in well-drained but moisture-retentive soil and keep well watered, especially in dry spells. Dead-head regularly. Discard plants after flowering.

VARIETIES 'Blue Gem', small, sky-blue flowers; 'Carnival Mixed' (*above*), a compact strain at 23cm/9in high, in red, white, cream, yellow, orange, bronze and blue.

POSSIBLE PROBLEMS Foot rot or root rot infection may cause plants to collapse at ground level.

▨ CUT FLOWER TIP

With its cloudy mass of tiny flowers, this is a must for flower arrangers as a background for more dramatic blooms; it is very effective at softening what might otherwise be a rather stark or formal arrangement. It is best to cut blooms early in the morning or last thing at night, and place in water immediately.

▨ PLANTING TIP

These flowers make ideal pot plants for the conservatory or greenhouse. Do not allow roots to become dry. Pinch out to encourage bushiness.

PETUNIA

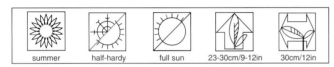

summer	half-hardy	full sun	23-30cm/9-12in	30cm/12in

Summer bedding would not be the same without the trumpet-shaped flowers of petunia hybrids providing a focus of colour that is vivid without being gaudy. Ideal for window-boxes and tubs, the trailing varieties combine particularly well with lobelia, alyssum, fuchsias and pelargoniums.

PROPAGATION Sow seed in early spring under protection with gentle heat. Prick the seedlings out into boxes when they are large enough to handle and harden off before planting out in late spring.

GROWING Petunias like reasonably fertile, free-draining soil and a warm, sunny position. Give them an occasional high-potash feed. Water regularly, especially if in containers, and remove faded flowerheads regularly. Discard after flowering.

VARIETIES Numerous named hybrids are available. Multifloras bear a profusion of 5cm/2in blooms; Grandifloras carry fewer, but larger, flowers. 'Resisto Mixed' (*above*): multifloras, red, pink, yellow, white, blue; 'Multiflora Double Mixed', large frilled flowers; 'Super Fanfare Mixed', grandifloras, double flowers.

POSSIBLE PROBLEMS Aphids on young shoots

MOLUCELLA

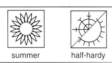

summer	half-hardy	full sun	60-90cm/2-3ft	30cm/12in

A particular favourite with flower arrangers, *Molucella laevis* or bells-of-Ireland should not be overlooked as a useful addition to the summer border. Its green spires add height and provide the perfect foil for more showy plants. Each tiny white flower is surrounded by a light green, bowl-shaped calyx. No named varieties are available.

PROPAGATION Sow seed under protection in early spring. Harden the seedlings off before planting out in late spring. In favoured locations seed may be sown directly into the flowering site in spring and the seedlings thinned to 23cm/9in apart when they are large enough to handle.

GROWING Ordinary well-drained loam is best. Give molucellas a sheltered site. Pull up and discard plants after flowering.

POSSIBLE PROBLEMS Generally trouble-free.

▨ ORGANIC TIP

Annuals like these are ideal for attracting beneficial insects into the garden, including bees for pollination. (Pollen is transferred from flower to flower by insects in search of nectar. The pollen sticks to the insect, and is then rubbed off on the next flower it visits on it's search for food.

▨ DRIED FLOWER TIP

The intriguing green flowers of this plant are excellent for drying, to provide winter colour in the home. For best results, cut just before the flowers open.

GODETIA

| summer | hardy | full sun | 30-60cm/12-24in | 15cm/6in |

These Californian natives produce brightly coloured flowers for the summer border or for cutting. The plants are compact, with mid-green, pointed leaves, and bear trumpet-shaped blooms of red, cerise, peach or pink, often edged with white. The best-known species, *Godetia amoena whitneyi*, syn. *G. grandiflora*, is often listed under clarkia in gardening catalogues.

PROPAGATION Sow seeds outside in spring if they are to flower the same year. Thin seedlings to 15cm/6in apart. Sow in early autumn for flowering the following year. Protect with cloches in colder areas and do not thin the plants until the spring.

GROWING Godetias do best in light soils. Over-rich soil encourages leaf production at the expense of flowers.

VARIETIES 'Azalea-flowered Mixed' , semi-double flowers with frilled petals; 'Sybil Sherwood', salmon pink; 'Crimson Glow' (*above*), dwarf variety; 'Double White', large white flowers with golden eye.

POSSIBLE PROBLEMS Stem and root rot may cause the plants to collapse.

LOBELIA

| spring/autumn | half-hardy | full sun | 15cm/6in | 23cm/9in |

Lobelia erinus, a perennial treated as an annual, is an indispensable element in summer bedding schemes, while the trailing varieties are invaluable in window boxes and hanging baskets. Their diminutive size and intense colours – blue, magenta or bright white – make lobelias good companions for petunias, pelargoniums, French marigolds and fuchsias.

PROPAGATION Sow seed in pans under protection and with gentle heat in late winter. Prick out the tiny seedlings in groups of 3 or 4 into trays and grow on until all danger of frost has passed. Plant out in early summer.

GROWING Annual lobelias like light, free-draining soil. If grown in containers, be careful not to let the soil dry out.

VARIETIES 'Cambridge Blue', compact, pale blue flowers, light green foliage; 'Crystal Palace', compact, dark blue flowers, bronze foliage; 'Rosamund', carmine-red, white centre; 'Snowball', white.

POSSIBLE PROBLEMS Damping-off and root rot may cause plants to collapse.

▦ SPECIAL CARE TIP

Black root rot occurs when the same type of plants are always grown in the same bed. Avoid this and plant tagetes or calendula nearby to prevent attack by aphids.

▦ PLANTING TIP

Plant trailing lobelia in a hanging basket for an eye-catching display. In hot weather syringe with water every evening and soak the basket to a once a week.

LOBULARIA

| summer | half-hardy | full sun | 10cm/4in | 30cm/12in |

Lobularia maritima is a close relative of alyssum, which it closely resembles, bearing masses of tiny sweetly scented flowers. This dwarf plant is often used in summer bedding schemes, window boxes and hanging baskets, in company with lobelia. It is also suitable for rock gardens and will grow in the crevices of paving or as an edging.

PROPAGATION Sow seeds under glass in early spring. Prick out young plants and harden off before planting out in early summer. If sowing outdoors where the plants are to grow, wait until late spring and thin seedlings to 15cm/6in intervals when they are large enough to handle. Garden plants sometimes self-seed.

GROWING Remove dead flowers regularly with sharp scissors and flowering will continue for 2-4 months.

VARIETIES Choose named varieties such as 'Rosie O'Day' (*above*), rose-pink; 'Little Dorrit', white, also known as 'Little Gem'; 'Lilac Queen' and 'Violet Queen'.

POSSIBLE PROBLEMS Generally trouble-free.

CALLISTEPHUS

| summer/autumn | half-hardy | full sun | 60-75cm/24-30in | 30 cm/12in |

The China aster, *Callistephus chinensis*, bears chrysanthemum-like blooms from high summer to the first frosts. They are bushy plants with flowers in all tones of pink, red and purple or white; they may be double, semi-double or single, pompon or feathered. The Duchess strain has thick, incurving petals.

PROPAGATION Sow seed outdoors where plants are to flower in late spring; thin seedlings to 30cm/12in apart when they are large enough to handle.

GROWING Light, free-draining soil is best, but any good garden soil will do. Choose a site protected from wind. Stake the taller varieties before the flowers open. Dead-head regularly for successive flowering. China asters are susceptible to wilt; to prevent the occurrence of this disease, do not grow them on the same plot for 2 consecutive years.

VARIETIES 'Miss Europe', ball type, pink; 'Fire Devil', Duchess strain, wilt-resistant, bright scarlet; the Giants of California strain has large, ruffled flowers; 'Milady', dwarf selection in numerous colours.

POSSIBLE PROBLEMS Wilt causes plants to collapse; cucumber mosaic virus causes yellow mottling of leaves.

▩ PLANTING TIP

This is a very reliable carpeting plant for tubs, dry-stone walls, paving, or rockeries, providing a mass of tiny flowers. To plant in a wall, or in a crack in paving stones, wrap the roots in a piece of old turf well soaked in water and insert in a prepared hole.

▩ PLANTING TIP

The dwarf varieties are excellent for growing in tubs or containers on a patio or balcony, where you can provide a sheltered site protected from the wind. Callistephus will bring a splash of colour to the garden in late summer and early autumn when many other plants look tired. Dead-head regularly.

Nigella

| summer | hardy | full sun | 15-45cm/6-18in | 23cm/9in |

Popularly known as love-in-a-mist, *Nigella damascena* is one of the group of plants typical of the English cottage garden. It looks well with lupins and aquilegias against a background of clematis and old roses. The leaves are delicate and fern-like; the flowers, usually blue but sometimes pink, resemble cornflowers.

PROPAGATION Sow seeds in the flowering site at intervals throughout the spring. Protect with cloches in colder areas. Thin out to 20cm/8in apart when the seedlings are large enough to handle. Love-in-a-mist does not transplant well.

GROWING A well-drained soil is best, and a position in full sun essential. Plants often self-seed, giving you new plants in succeeding years (though not necessarily where you would choose to put them).

VARIETIES 'Miss Jekyll', bright blue semi-double flowers; 'Persian Jewels', mixed colours – pink, red, mauve, ꜰ ꞁle, blue and white.

POSSIBLE PROBLEMS Generally trouble-free.

Myosotis

| spring | hardy | semi-shade | 30cm/12in | 15cm/6in |

This biennial member of the forget-me-not family bears sprays of tiny, fragrant blue flowers that provide drifts of colour in the border. They can be naturalized in woodland or raised under glass for cut flowers.

PROPAGATION Sow seed outdooors in a seed bed in late spring; thin the seedlings to 15cm/6in when they are large enough to handle. Transfer to the growing site in early autumn for flowering the following spring. Plants grown under glass should be transferred to 7.5cm/ 3in pots of compost. They need no winter heat and should flower up to 6 weeks earlier than those outdoors.

GROWING Forget-me-nots are not fussy plants, but do best in semi-shade in moisture-retentive soil that has been previously enriched with well-rotted compost or leaf mould.

VARIETIES 'Blue Bird', deep blue flowers; hybrids with *M. alpestris* include 'Carmine King', deep pink, 'Marine', clear blue and 'White Ball'.

POSSIBLE PROBLEMS Plants may die in soil that becomes waterlogged in winter.

▦ DRIED FLOWER TIP

The sky-blue, saucer-shaped flowers, surrounded by feathery foliage, are excellent for cutting, but leave some to develop into seed. The striking seed pods, green with maroon stripes, look well in dried flower arrangements. Cut the pods when swollen, tie in loose bundles and hang in warm air to dry.

▦ PLANTING TIP

Good in the herbaceous border, these tiny blue flowers are also useful for planting in bare rose beds to bring colour before the roses begin to bloom.

CONVOLVULUS

summer	hardy	full sun	30cm/12in	15cm/6in

Mediterranean in origin, *Convolvulus tricolor* is a garden relative of bindweed, though happily much less rampant. Like its other familiar cousin, ipomoea (morning glory), it bears open, trumpet-shaped blue flowers which appear throughout the summer and (unlike morning glory) stay open all day.

PROPAGATION Sow seed in the open in spring, covering with cloches to protect from cold until the plants are established. Thin seedlings to 12cm/5in when they reach 5cm/2in in height.

GROWING Give *C. tricolor* a sheltered site on ordinary, well-drained soil. Keep the young plants free of weeds. Remove faded flowerheads to ensure a succession of blooms.

VARIETIES 'Blue Flash' (*above*), dwarf variety, bushy plants, deep blue flower with yellow and white eye; 'Crimson Monarch', cherry-red flowers; 'Sky Blue', light blue.

DELPHINIUM

summer	hardy	sun/semi-shade	30cm-1.2m/1-4ft	30cm/12in

There are two types of annual delphiniums, namely *D. ajacis*, known as rocket larkspur, and *D. consolida*, the common larkspur. Both are typical cottage garden plants, their tall spikes clothed with flowers of blue, white, pink or purple. They bring height and grace to the summer border, and are suitable as cut flowers.

PROPAGATION Sow seed directly in the growing site in successive sowings throughout the spring. Thin the seedlings to about 30cm/12in depending on variety. Alternatively sow seed in the autumn and protect with cloches over winter.

GROWING Delphiniums need well-cultivated, fertile soil and a site sheltered from wind. Provide twiggy sticks for support for taller varieties.

VARIETIES *D. ajacis*, Hyacinth-flowered types: thickly set, double flowers, on blunt stems up to 60cm/24in high; *D. consolida*, Giant imperials: up to 1.2m/4ft, branching out from the base; Stock-flowered types: up to 90cm/3ft, best for cutting.

POSSIBLE PROBLEMS Slugs and snails damage young shoots. Crown, root and stem rot cause plants to collapse. Cucumber mosaic virus shows as mottled leaves.

▨ ORGANIC TIP

Plant in or near the rose bed or vegetable garden to help minimize aphid attacks: the open flowers attract hoverflies whose larvae eat greenfly.

▨ PLANTING TIP

In order to allow sufficient room between plants the rule is usually that the distance between plants should be equal to their height when fully grown.

However, you can vary this rule for very tall plants with small leaves, like delphiniums. Plant them the equivalent of half their finished height apart.

LUNARIA

| spring/summer | hardy | semi-shade | 60-90cm/2-3ft | 30cm/12in |

No flower arranger's garden is complete without honesty, grown less for its purple flowers than the silvery round seed pods that follow. The biennial *Lunaria annua (above)* is the best choice as the perennial variety *L. rediviva* self-seeds very easily and may become invasive.

PROPAGATION Sow seeds in an outdoor seedbed from spring to mid-summer. Thin the seedlings to 15cm/6in when they are large enough to handle. Transplant to the growing site in early autumn to flower the following spring.

GROWING Any soil will do. If collecting stems with seed pods for drying, pick in late summer before they are damaged by cold winds.

VARIETIES 'Munstead Purple', tall rose-purple flowers; 'Variegata', crimson flowers, silver-spotted leaves. Mixed varieties are available.

POSSIBLE PROBLEMS Club root causes distortion of roots but does not affect the visible part of the plant. If it occurs, do not use the same site for honesty (or any member of the cabbage family) for three years.

ASPERULA

| summer | hardy | semi-shade | 15-23cm/6-9in | 15-23cm/6-9in |

Asperula orientalis is a neat, low-growing plant with attractive star-shaped leaves and clusters of tiny blue flowers that are lightly scented. Good at the front of the border or for cutting, this species may also be grown as a pot plant. No named varieties are available.

PROPAGATION Sow seed outdoors in late spring directly in the flowering site. Thin seedlings in two stages to a final spacing of 10-15cm/4-6in. For pot plants, sow under glass in early autumn, placing 5 seeds to a 12.5cm/5in pot of compost, and overwinter in gentle heat.

GROWING Asperulas do best in moist soil. When the plants are 10cm/4in high, stake them with twiggy branches for support. Discard plants after flowering.

POSSIBLE PROBLEMS Generally trouble-free.

■ DRIED FLOWER TIP

The white central wall of the seed pod is the part used for dried arrangements: the outside part should be carefully stripped off.

■ ORGANIC TIP

The common form of asperula – A. odorata – is also known as sweet woodruff and is sometimes grown as a herb. The flowering stems are used medicinally, as they have sedative, diuretic and antispasmodic properties. The dried leaves and stems are used to make a herbal tea.

DIANTHUS

summer	hardy	full sun	30-60cm/12-24in	25cm/10in

Although this member of the dianthus family is a perennial, *D. barbatus*, or sweet william, gives best results when grown as a biennial. The dense flat heads of fragrant flowers range in colour from white through pink to deep cherry red. Some are marked with concentric rings of a contrasting colour. They look best grown in groups in the border, and are very popular as cut flowers.

PROPAGATION Sow seed under glass in early spring at 13°C/55°F. When large enough to handle, prick out seedlings into boxes at 7.5cm/3in apart and grow on at 10°C/50°F. Harden off and plant out in the flowering site in early summer.

GROWING A position in full sun is best, in ordinary, well-drained alkaline soil. Dress acid soils with lime before planting out.

VARIETIES There are no named varieties of sweet william, but hybrids known as 'Sweet Wivelsfield' bearing larger flower-heads have been developed.

POSSIBLE PROBLEMS Carnation ring spot causes deformed plants. Brown spots on leaves are caused by leaf spot.

CENTAUREA

summer	hardy	sun	90 cm/3ft	30cm/12in

Centaurea cyanus, the cornflower, is a sturdy border plant with blooms of pure blue, pink or white that make excellent cut flowers. Its cousin sweet sultan, *C. moschata*, reaches only 60cm/24in and bears fragrant flowers of white, yellow, pink or deep purple.

PROPAGATION Sow seeds in the open where they are to grow in spring, or in the autumn with the protection of cloches over winter for early flowering the following year. Thin the seedlings to 23cm/9in apart.

GROWING Any fertile, well-drained soil is suitable. Choose a site protected from winds and give taller varieties the support of twiggy sticks. Dead-head regularly to encourage prolonged flowering.

VARIETIES *C. cyanus*: 'Dwarf Blue' (*above*); 'Polka Dot' includes a variety of col-ours; 'Dwarf Rose Gem' is a compact pink-flowered variety good for growing in pots. *C. moschata*: no named varieties, but *C. m. imperialis* is a reliable form with large flowers.

POSSIBLE PROBLEMS Petal blight; rust.

▨ PROPAGATION TIP

These are quite easy to propagate from non-flowering side-shoots in early summer. Strip foliage from the lower section of the cutting, and dip end in hor- mone rooting powder. Fill a seed box or small pots with sandy soil or potting compost, make a suitable hole with a dibber and firm in each cutting.

▨ ORGANIC TIP

An ideal plant for attracting insects. The flowers provide a good supply of nectar, especially for bees, whose long tongues can easily reach the nectar source.

ANTIRRHINUM

| summer | hardy | full sun | 10-90cm/4-36in | 23-45cm/9-18in |

Commonly known as snapdragon, *Antirrhinum majus* is a perennial usually treated as an annual, although in very favoured areas it may survive the winter. Modern varieties are available in all colours except blue, and the profuse tubular flowers look stunning in a summer border. They also make good cut flowers.

PROPAGATION Sow seeds in very early spring indoors with gentle heat. Prick the seedlings out into boxes when they are large enough to handle and harden off before planting out in late spring. Alternatively raise plants during the summer in a cold frame for planting out the following year.

GROWING A well-drained soil, previously enriched with well-rotted compost, is best. Pinch out growing tips to encourage bushy growth, unless single stems are required for cutting. Dead-head regularly.

VARIETIES Always choose rust-resistant varieties from the following divisions. 'Maximum', up to 90cm/3ft, many colours – the Rocket group is a vigorous strain; 'Nanum', up to 45cm/18in – 'Cheerio' is a sturdy hybrid; 'Pumilum', dwarfs at 15cm/6in. 'Tom Thumb Mixed' and 'Pixie' are reliable types which may also be grown in the rock garden.

POSSIBLE PROBLEMS Rust is the major problem. Aphids may damage young shoots.

ORGANIC TIP

This popular border plant is also an ideal choice for the organic garden, since the sweet scent of the pouch-shaped flowers will attract bees. Plant in a sunny border to ensure that it continues flowering throughout the summer.

LATHYRUS

| summer | hardy | full sun | 3m/10ft | 15-30cm/6-12 in |

The sweet pea, *Lathyrus odoratus*, climbs by means of leaf tendrils. Its wing-petalled flowers are coloured white, pink, red, lilac or cream, and are sometimes strongly scented. They are extremely popular as cut flowers.

PROPAGATION Sowing can take place either in very early spring in a heated greenhouse or in late spring directly in the flowering site. To speed germination, soak the seeds in water for 12 hours before sowing. Prick out seedlings from early sowings into 7.5cm/3in pots and harden off before planting out in late spring. Plants may also be raised from summer sowings in a cold frame and set out the following year.

GROWING Sweet peas thrive on rich soil. Dig plenty of well-rotted compost or manure into the growing site before planting out. Provide pea sticks or posts and wires for support. Pinch out plants at 15cm/6in high to encourage side shoots. Pick the flowers regularly.

VARIETIES The popular Spencer group includes 'Swan Lake', white; 'Noel Sutton', deep blue; 'Leamington', lavender; 'Princess Elizabeth', coral pink and cream; 'Carlotta', carmine red. 'Knee-Hi', dwarf type, supported with light brushwood makes a bush about 1.2 x 1.2m/4 x 4ft, many colours available.

POSSIBLE PROBLEMS Slugs on leaves; mildew may occur.

CUT FLOWER TIP

They are ready for cutting when the bottom bloom on each stem is in full colour. If not cut, remove the flowers as they fade to encourage new growth.

SCHIZANTHUS

summer	half-hardy	full sun	45-60cm/18-24in	20cm/8in

Schizanthus are erect plants with delicate light green foliage, bearing a profusion of orchid-like blooms throughout the summer. Flowers may be pink, salmon, red, yellow or white and their fluttering petals have given rise to the popular name butterfly flower. They do well in tubs and as cut flowers.

PROPAGATION Sow seeds under protection at 16-18°C/60-65°F in early spring. Prick out the seedlings into 7.5cm/3in pots when they are large enough to handle and harden off before planting out in late spring 10-15cm/4-6in apart. Alternatively sow directly into the flowering site in mid-spring, thinning the seedlings to the recommended planting distances when large enough.

GROWING Soil that has previously been enriched with well-rotted organic matter gives best results. A position in full sun is essential for sturdy plants. Pinch out tips of young plants to encourage bushy growth and stake with split canes if necessary. Discard the plants after flowering.

VARIETIES Choose varieties of the hybrid S. × wisetonensis such as 'Butterfly': pink or white, large flowers, or 'Star Parade': compact form, all colours.

POSSIBLE PROBLEMS Aphids may damage growing tips.

ORGANIC TIP

Avoid attack from aphids by planting beside tagetes, papaver or nasturtiums. These attract hoverflies whose larvae eat large quantities of aphids.

CHRYSANTHEMUM

summer	hardy	full sun	60-90cm/2-3 ft	25cm/10in

Chrysanthemums comprise a huge family of very varied plants. The most popular annual variety, *Chrysanthemum carinatum*, has bright green, coarsely dissected leaves and cheerful daisy-like blooms 5cm/2in or more across. Petals yellow at the base and banded in pink and white, red or purple radiate from a flat, purple, central disc. Double-flowered versions are available. The species C. coronarium has a yellow centre and yellow and white flowers. C maximum (above) has single white flowers with yellow centres and toothed leaves. Annual chrysanthemums prolong the life of the summer border by flowering well into the autumn.

PROPAGATION Sow seed directly into the flowering site towards the end of spring, and thin the seedlings to 25cm/10in when large enough to handle. In warmer areas, an autumn sowing – protected with cloches over winter – gives large, earlier blooms the following year.

GROWING Chrysanthemums like fertile, well-drained soil and a sunny position. Pinch out the first growing tips to encourage long side stems for cutting. Although the stems are strong, supporting canes may be advisable on windy sites.

VARIETIES 'Monarch Court Jesters', many colours, single flowers; 'Flore-Plenum', yellow/white, compact double flowers

POSSIBLE PROBLEMS Aphids and earwigs can be problems.

ORGANIC TIP

To avoid damage by earwigs, set a traditional trap. Place a flower pot filled with dried grass or straw upside down on a cane near the flower heads.

The earwigs, which are nocturnal creatures, will crawl into the pot to avoid daylight - simply remove the pot once a week and burn the grass or straw.

ZINNIA

summer	half-hardy	full sun	60cm/24in	30cm/12in

The most popular annual zinnia, *Zinnia elegans*, is native to Mexico; the vivid colours of its luxurious blooms certainly have an exotic air. The species is bright purple, but its varieties include yellow, pink, scarlet, orange, white, lavender and violet; some are double-flowered, others are banded in a contrasting colour.

PROPAGATION Sow seed under protection at 16-18°C/60-64°F in early spring. When the seedlings are large enough to handle, prick them out into small peat or fibre pots so that the roots will not be disturbed when transplanting. Harden off before planting out in late spring.

GROWING Zinnias like free-draining, fertile soil and a sunny, sheltered site. Pinch out the growing shoots on young plants to encourage a bushy shape. Remove faded or rain-damaged flowerheads.

VARIETIES Dahlia-flowered strain: 'Giant Double Mixed' (*above*), double flowers, all colours; 'Canary Bird', yellow; 'Envy', lime green. Burpee hybrids, double flowers with wavy petals, are available in all colours. Varieties of the 'Pumila' type are only 15cm/6in high: 'Early Wonder' is a good mixture.

POSSIBLE PROBLEMS Cucumber mosaic virus causes mottled leaves.

SALPIGLOSSIS

summer/autumn	half-hardy	full sun	45-60cm/18-24in	30cm/12in

Salpiglossis sinuata is such an exotic-looking plant that it is difficult to believe it is so easy to grow – or that it belongs to the same family of plants as the potato. Sometimes called painted tongue, sometimes the velvet trumpet flower, its tall, graceful, slightly sticky stems are clothed with narrow leaves and crowned with blooms all summer long. The colour range includes red, pink, orange, gold, yellow or blue, streaked with a contrasting colour.

PROPAGATION Sow seeds in late spring directly in the flowering site and thin seedlings to 25cm/10in apart when large enough to handle.

GROWING Salpiglossis are unfussy about soil type, as long as it is reasonably fertile. An open, sunny site is best, though in exposed positions stems will need the support of split canes. Remove dead flower spikes regularly.

VARIETIES 'Splash', compact plants, early flowering, many colours.

POSSIBLE PROBLEMS Aphids may infest the stems. Foot or root rot causes plants to collapse.

ORGANIC TIP

Dig compost into the herbaceous border in early spring. After planting, mulch with well-rotted manure or compost to help conserve moisture.

SPECIAL CARE TIP

This exotic plant comes originally from the Andes. It does need a sunny, sheltered position – if conditions are not suitable, you could consider growing this in the conservatory or greenhouse, where it will provide a bright splash of colour, or in a sheltered spot on a patio or balcony.

SALVIA

| summer | half-hardy | full sun | 15-35cm/6-14in | 25-30cm/10-12in |

The genus *Salvia* includes a number of species, among them the herbs sage and clary. *S. splendens*, a perennial grown as an annual, is an established favourite in summer bedding schemes, especially of the formal type. Its dense spikes of true scarlet flowers last into early autumn. Modern varieties include pink, purple and white-flowering forms.

PROPAGATION Sow seeds in pans in early spring at 18°C/64°F and prick the seedlings out into boxes when they are large enough to handle. Harden off in a cold frame before planting out in late spring.

GROWING Salvias need a warm, open, sunny site on moderately rich, free-draining soil. Do not let them dry out in hot weather. Remove faded flowerheads regularly.

VARIETIES 'Blaze of Fire', 'Tetra Scarlet', both early flowering; 'Tom Thumb', only 20cm/8in high, red or white; 'Dress Parade', all colours.

POSSIBLE PROBLEMS Low temperatures inhibit growth, causing stunted plants and yellowing leaves.

ESCHSCHOLZIA

| summer | hardy | full sun | 30-60cm/12-24in | 15cm/6in |

Eschscholzia californica, the Californian poppy, is a dazzling candidate for the summer border, especially on dry soils. It blazes with colour – red, orange, yellow or pink – right through to the autumn. The flowers are followed by cylindrical seed pods, 7.5cm/3in long and blue-green in colour.

PROPAGATION Successive sowings ensure a long flowering season. Sow seeds in the flowering site at 2-week intervals throughout the spring, thinning the seedlings to 15cm/6in when they are large enough to handle. Alternatively, sow in early autumn and protect with cloches over winter for flowering the following year.

GROWING For brightly coloured blooms a poor, sandy soil is best. Flowers required for cutting should be picked when in bud. Self-sown seedlings do well in succeeding years.

VARIETIES 'Ballerina', mixed colours, semi-double flowers with fluted petals; 'Mission Bells', mixed colours, only 23cm/9in high; 'Harlequin Hybrids' *(above)*.

POSSIBLE PROBLEMS Generally trouble-free.

▨ PLANTING TIP

Practise companion planting to avoid aphids, which spread diseases as they feed on neighbouring plants. Remove any diseased leaves immediately.

▨ PLANTING TIP

If space is limited, it is worth remembering that this plant has a tendency to overrun the garden, if it gets the chance. Self-sown seedlings do well, thriving even on poor soils. To avoid self-seeding, dead-head the plants regularly and do not allow the seed pods (which look very attractive) to form.

AGERATUM

| summer | half-hardy | full sun | 12-30cm/5-12in | 15-30cm/6-12in |

Ageratum houstonianum is a native of Mexico and is sometimes listed as *A. mexicanum*. It produces mounds of small, soft-looking, daisy-like flowers amid heart-shaped leaves. It is an excellent choice for edging or for the front of the border, since the blue, white or pink flowers bloom from early summer through to autumn.

PROPAGATION Sow seeds in gentle heat in early spring and prick the seedlings off into boxes at 5cm/2in apart when they are large enough to handle. Harden off before planting out in early summer.

GROWING A well-drained fertile soil is best. Water the plants well in dry weather and dead-head regularly to ensure a succession of blooms.

VARIETIES Choose F_1 hybrids such as 'Blue Surf', 'Fairy Pink' or 'Summer Snow'.

POSSIBLE PROBLEMS Foot rot and root rot may occur, causing plants to collapse.

LAVATERA

| summer | hardy | full sun | 60cm/24in | 45cm/18in |

Lavatera trimestris is an annual cousin of the perennial mallow, with larger flowers – they may be 10cm/4in across – which are excellent for cutting. Both pink and white forms are available. Lavatera makes a beautiful bushy plant whose long flowering period well justifies a place in the border.

PROPAGATION Sow seed in the flowering site in spring, or in the autumn for flowering the following year. Thin the seedlings to 45cm/18in apart when they are large enough to handle.

GROWING Light, well-drained soil is preferred. An over-rich soil will encourage foliage at the expense of flowers. Stake young plants with twiggy branches when they reach 10cm/4in in height. Discard plants after flowering.

VARIETIES 'Silver Cup' (*above*), bright pink; 'Mont Blanc', white.

POSSIBLE PROBLEMS Leaf spot and rust may occur.

■ PLANTING TIP

Ageratums are among the few annual bedding plants that will tolerate dry soil and light shade. As well as planting in the border, use them to make a colourful carpet of flowers around the base of trees and large shrubs, where other plants will not thrive.

■ SPECIAL CARE TIP

This is a tender flower, so plant in a sunny, sheltered position, especially in cooler regions or exposed gardens. Protect from cold, drying winds.

Mentzelia

summer	hardy	sun	45cm/18in	23cm/9in

A native of California, *Mentzelia lindleyi* is distinguished by stunning, bright yellow flowers 5cm/2in wide with glossy heart-shaped petals. Numerous fine gold stamens cluster in the centre of each flower. Lightly scented, mentzelias make a vivid splash of colour in the summer border. They are also known as *Bartonia aurea*. No named varieties of the species are available.

PROPAGATION Sow seeds directly in the flowering site in spring and thin the seedlings to 23cm/ 9in apart when they are large enough to handle.

GROWING Mentzelias do best on well-drained fertile soil into which well-rotted organic matter has previously been incorporated.

POSSIBLE PROBLEMS Generally trouble-free.

Mesembryanthemum

summer	hardy	sun	15cm/6in	15cm/6in

Commonly known as the Livingstone daisy, *Mesembryanthemum criniflorum* is a succulent, low-growing plant best as informal edging for the summer border or in the rock garden. The small but vivid flowers may be apricot, pink, magenta, orange or white; they only open in full sun. The correct botanical name is now *Dorotheanthus bellidiflorus*. No named varieties of the species are available.

PROPAGATION Sow the seeds under protection and with gentle heat in early spring. Prick the seedlings off into boxes when they are large enough to handle and harden off in a cold frame before planting out in late spring. Seeds may also be sown directly into the flowering site in mid-spring, thinning seedlings to 30cm/12in.

GROWING Any well-drained soil will do, but light sandy soils are preferred.

POSSIBLE PROBLEMS Foot rot may cause plants to collapse at ground level.

ORGANIC TIP

Supply enough nutrients by digging in well-rotted manure or compost in early spring and give the border a dressing of fish, blood and bone meal before planting.

SPECIAL CARE TIP

Although this plant is easy to grow, it is susceptible to foot rot, shown by blackening of the stem base before the plants collapse. Foot rot is often caused by waterlogged ground, so make sure that drainage is adequate. If your soil is unsuitable, grow this plant on a rockery, where drainage will be better.

PERENNIALS

The term perennial is used to describe any long-lived plant that is non-woody (as shrubs and trees are). Herbaceous perennials are those that die down in the autumn and reappear in spring.

This is a large, diverse and useful group of plants. It would be easy to fill your garden with nothing but perennials and still have plants of all shapes, sizes and colours. This was the principle behind the nineteenth-century herbaceous border, which – though stunningly beautiful from late spring to late summer – had the disadvantage of descending into dullness from late autumn to spring. The modern mixed border makes the most of the qualities of perennials while compensating for their shortcomings with shrubs, bulbs, annuals and biennials. Unlike the herbaceous borders of old, which were traditionally rectangular but very large – often 3 m/10 ft deep and three times as long – the mixed border can be irregular in shape. Today curved lines are preferred to strict symmetry except in the most formal settings. Borders are smaller and, where space permits, island beds in the middle of lawns are popular. Again, curved lines are preferable; an indented oval is a pleasing shape and one which makes it easy to get close to plants that need attention. In any but the narrowest borders, it is a good idea to set stepping stones into the soil here and there to enable you to approach plants at the back for staking, dead-heading and other routine tasks like cutting down the stems after flowering and division when necessary. Bear in mind the space that most perennials need, and do not try to cramp them in too small an area. If your border is very narrow, dwarf shrubs, bulbs and a climber at the back might be a better combination.

The long life of most perennials is what makes them an attractive proposition to today's busy gardeners. Perennials are a more or less permanent fixture, with the exception of some short-lived species like delphiniums and hollyhocks (*Althaea rosea*), which need replacing after about five years. Because of this longevity perennials should be chosen and sited with almost as much care as you would bestow upon a shrub or tree. This applies particularly to species like peonies and Christmas roses (*Helleborus niger*), which greatly resent disturbance but, if left alone, will bloom through countless seasons. Other species, by contrast, need to be divided regularly not only for propagation purposes but to look their best. Astilbe, coreopsis and viola fall into this category.

CHOOSING PERENNIALS When designing a flowerbed where the principal elements are perennial, it is useful to make a plan on paper (*see page 12*). This will enable you to site plants of different heights and colours in a pleasing relation to each other, bearing in mind flowering time, the ultimate spread of the plants and their particular requirements as to site and soil. Always set perennials the correct distance apart, and if the bare space between them when they are young and small displeases you, fill it up with annuals. Eventually the perennials will fill up the gaps. Indeed, many make excellent ground cover plants, giving a luxurious effect

and smothering weeds. Some perennials which perform this function are bergenia, brunnera, *Euphorbia robbiae*, *Geranium endressii*, pulmonaria and stokesia.

Because flower colour is the single most important factor affecting choice of plants, the entries in this book have been arranged in colour groups as far as possible. Other design considerations to be taken into account are height and quality of foliage. Tall plants which should be situated at the back of the border or towards the centres of an island bed are some campanulas, delphiniums, echinops, hollyhocks, lupins and mallow (*Malva alcea*). A border should be twice as wide as the tallest plant in it. The middle range includes *Alchemilla mollis*, astilbe, catananche, *Monarda didyma*, peonies, poppies and trollius. At the front of the border you might place low-growing plants such as *Bellis perennis*, *Oenethera missouriensis*, dwarf coreopsis, geraniums, potentilla, polyanthus, *Stokesia laevis* and violas. Alchemilla, euphorbia, pulmonaria, bergenia and brunnera are among perennials prized for their foliage.

Sedum spectabile, *in the foreground, is a striking border plant with year-round interest derived from its attractive grey-green leaves.*

Hardy perennials can be purchased in containers or bare root direct from the nursery or garden centre. The planting procedure is identical whichever way they arrive. Dig a hole with a trowel or spade about one and a half times as large as the root ball. Set the plant in the hole so that its crown (the point at which the annual stems arise) is about 2.5cm/1in below the surrounding soil surface. Fill in around the roots and firm with fists or feet, depending on the size of the plant. To save on expensive garden centre bills, ask your friends and neighbours if you can take cuttings or make divisions from their perennials to establish in your own garden.

The choice of perennials is so wide that they can be used to contribute to any type of garden design – there is undoubtedly a perennial for every situation. It is this versatility that makes them the most valuable group of plants.

ALCHEMILLA

| summer | hardy | sun/semi-shade | 30-45cm/12-18in | 60cm/24in |

Commonly known as lady's mantle, *Alchemilla mollis* (*above*) is less valued for its flowers than its handsome leaves, which are light green, palmate and particularly attractive after rain when droplets settle on the leaves. Clusters of tiny, star-shaped lime-green flowers appear in early summer and are very long-lasting. These plants look their best at the front of a border. There are no named varieties of the species. *A. alpina*, at 15cm/6in, is a smaller species suitable for rock gardens.

GROWING Set out plants between autumn and spring when the weather is favourable. Alchemillas like moist, well-drained soil and a position in sun or partial shade. Set twigs around the plants for support and cut the stems right back after flowering.

PROPAGATION Divide established plants in autumn or spring. Plants usually produce numerous self-sown seedlings which do well.

POSSIBLE PROBLEMS Generally trouble-free.

EUPHORBIA

| spring/summer | hardy | semi-shade | 60cm/ 24in | 90cm/3ft |

The euphorbia family comprises a great many plants including annuals and shrubs. Among the evergreen perennials *E. robbiae* (*above*) is particularly attractive, with upright stems, whorls of dark green leaves and loose heads of lime-green flowers and bracts. It makes excellent ground cover under trees. Plants like euphorbias and alchemillas (*see left*) are invaluable elements in a garden design where patches of green are used as a foil for the bright colours of summer flowers. There are no named varieties of this species.

GROWING Set out young plants in spring, in light, well-drained soil. While most evergreen euphorbias tolerate some shade, *E. robbiae* will thrive even in full shade. Exposed windy sites are not suitable. Remove flowerheads when the colour fades. Cut plants back in late summer to keep them bushy.

PROPAGATION Take 7.5cm/3in basal cuttings in spring and insert in a peat/sand mixture in a cold frame. Plant out when rooted. Divide established plants between autumn and spring.

POSSIBLE PROBLEMS Cold winds and frosts may damage young shoots.

▓ PLANTING TIP

The light green flowers and leaves of this plant provide a striking contrast to other, more colourful flowers in a border. Try combining them with orange or golden-coloured lilies for an eye-catching display. This plant is popular with flower arrangers on account of its unusual colouring and can also be used dried.

▓ CUT FLOWER TIP

This tall attractive plant is a good choice for flower arranging, as the dark leaves and lime-green flowers contrast effectively with bright flowers.

DICENTRA

spring/summer	hardy	semi-shade	45-60cm/18-24in	45cm/18in

Dicentras make excellent plants for the border, and by growing two or three different species you can be assured of flowers from spring to late summer. All have fern-like foliage and slender stems bearing nodding flowers of white, pale pink or rose red.

GROWING Set out young plants from autumn to early spring, taking great care not to damage the fragile roots. Soil should be moisture-retentive but well-drained and, for best results, rich in humus. Apply a mulch of well-rotted organic matter each spring.

PROPAGATION Divide established plants between autumn and spring, or take root cuttings 7.5cm/3in long in early spring. Insert in a peat/sand mixture in a cold frame. When the young leaves are well formed, transfer to a nursery bed and grow on until transplanting to the permanent site in autumn.

SPECIES *D. formosa*, large clusters of pink, white or red flowers, early summer; *D. spectabilis* (bleeding heart), arching stems of rose flowers in summer – 'Alba' (*above*) is a white form; *D. eximia*, only 30cm/12in high, rose pink or white flowers right through summer.

POSSIBLE PROBLEMS Generally trouble-free.

ACHILLEA

summer	hardy	full sun	60cm/24in	45cm/18in

The garden relatives of the common yarrow bear yellow or white flowers in flattened clusters. With fern-like, grey-green leaves, they are handsome additions to the summer border.

GROWING Set out young plants from autumn to spring in well-drained soil. Cut the stems back to ground level in late autumn each year.

PROPAGATION Divide established plants in spring into portions each bearing 4-5 young shoots and replant immediately.

VARIETIES *A. filipendula* 'Gold Plate', yellow flowers bloom all summer, good for dried flowers; *A.* × 'King Edward', forms low (10cm/4in high) hummocks of long-lasting primrose yellow flowers, suitable for rock gardens; *A.* × 'Moonshine' (*above*), feathery leaves, sharp yellow densely packed flowerheads; *A.* × *taygetea*, 45cm/18in high, pale yellow flowers 5-10cm/2-4in across, the best variety for cutting.

POSSIBLE PROBLEMS Generally trouble-free.

◼ SPECIAL CARE TIP

Does best in a semi-shaded spot with shelter from any cold winds. Enjoys wooded clearings where the young foliage will be protected from late frosts.

◼ DRIED FLOWER TIP

This is an easy and attractive plant to dry, with its flat flower-heads, which are generally white or yellow. Cut and tie in bunches and dry either from the roof of a shed, or in an indoor drying cupboard. The variety A. filipendulina holds its colour well, with masses of vivid yellow flowers.

OENOTHERA

| summer | hardy | full sun | 30-60cm/12-24in | 30-45cm/12-18in |

The oenothera family of North America includes the evening primrose, O. *biennis*. Most species bear yellow flowers, though some are white. Lightly scented, they are funnel-shaped at first but open almost flat. They bring prolonged and brilliant colour to the border, and because they self-seed freely are also good for wild gardens.

GROWING Set out small groups of young plants in the autumn, on light, free-draining soil. Oenotheras like an open, sunny site but will tolerate light shade. Water well in dry weather and dead-head regularly unless you want plants to self-seed. Cut down the stems after flowering.

PROPAGATION Divide established plants between autumn and spring. These perennials are short-lived but self-seed freely and successfully.

SPECIES O. *perennis*, syn. O. *pumila*, small, yellow flowers, pale green leaves, mid-summer; O. *missouriensis*, suitable for rock gardens or the front of the border at 15cm/6in high, abundant yellow flowers all summer; O. *fruticosa*, the variety 'Yellow River' bears a profusion of deep golden yellow flowers, mid-summer; O. *tetragona* 'Fireworks' (*above*) bears yellow flowers throughout the summer.

POSSIBLE PROBLEMS Heavy, waterlogged soil encourages root rot.

MECONOPSIS

| summer | hardy | semi-shade | 60cm/24in | 30cm/12in |

Meconopsis bear showy, poppy-like flowers in spring and summer on slender stems above neat rosettes of attractive leaves. They are beautiful plants for a mixed border.

GROWING A free-draining but moisture-retentive soil is essential, preferably non-alkaline. Meconopsis like a position in semi-shade and sheltered from wind. Water well in summer and support with pea sticks. Clear away old seedheads and foliage in late summer.

PROPAGATION Collect ripe seed from the plants in late summer and sow in a cold frame. Transfer the seedlings to boxes and keep over winter in a cold frame. Transplant to nursery rows until planting in the permanent site in the autumn.

SPECIES M. *cambrica* (Welsh poppy, *above*), vivid golden flowers in summer, self-seeds very freely, does not withstand hot summers; M. *betonicifolia* (Tibetan poppy), up to 90cm/3ft high, large, deep blue flowers in early summer, best choice for higher temperatures; M. *napaulensis*, up to 2m/6½ft high, with beautiful leaves and large blue, purple, red or pink flowers in early summer.

POSSIBLE PROBLEMS Downy mildew, black bean aphid.

ORGANIC TIP

Ideal for the organic garden as its night-scented flowers will attract moths from dusk onwards. Other insects will be attracted in daytime to the nectar.

SPECIAL CARE TIP

The Himalayan poppy was only recently brought to this country. It is a tall plant, with striking, blue flowers, and like other Asiatic species it should have a cool, partly shaded position, for example in a clearing among trees, in a lime-free soil kept moist with plenty of humus or well-rotted compost.

COREOPSIS

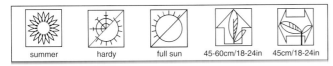

| summer | hardy | full sun | 45-60cm/18-24in | 45cm/18-24in |

Native to North America, the coreopsis is an accommodating plant, producing cheerful yellow star-shaped flowers throughout the summer even in polluted atmospheres.

GROWING Set out young plants between autumn and spring in well-drained, fertile soil. Chalky soils are tolerated. A position in full sun in an open border is preferred. Cut back some stems in late summer to encourage perennial growth.

PROPAGATION Divide established plants in early autumn or very early spring, making sure that each portion has 4-5 new shoots. Replant immediately. *C. grandiflora* can be increased by 7.5cm/3in basal cuttings taken in summer and rooted in a cold frame.

SPECIES *C. verticillata* (*above*), very fine leaves, a succession of star-shaped flowers 2.5cm/1in wide from mid to late summer; *C. grandiflora*, a short-lived perennial, up to 90cm/3ft high, bearing large daisy-like flowers all summer. This is the best species for cutting; named varieties include 'Mayfield Giant', 'Sunray', double flowers, and 'Goldfink', dwarf at 23cm/9in.

POSSIBLE PROBLEMS Froghoppers damage young shoots.

DORONICUM

| spring/summer | hardy | sun/semi-shade | 75cm/30in | 45cm/18in |

Commonly known as leopard's bane, doronicums bring the first glow of colour to the mixed border in spring, and if regularly dead-headed may produce a second flush of flowers in the autumn. The yellow, daisy-like flowers are excellent for cutting.

GROWING Set out young plants in the autumn, in fertile, moist soil in sun or dappled shade. Remove faded flowerheads regularly. Cut the stems back in autumn.

PROPAGATION Divide established plants in the autumn, using only the healthy outer portions. Replant immediately.

SPECIES *D. plantagineum* (*above*): vigorous plant, heart-shaped leaves, flowers 6.5cm/2½in across; good named varieties include 'Miss Mason' and 'Harpur Crewe'; *D. pardalianches* (great leopard's bane), up to 90cm/3ft high, requires staking; *D. cordatum*, only 20cm/8in but with golden yellow flowers 5cm/2in across.

POSSIBLE PROBLEMS Powdery mildew may appear on leaves.

■ CUT FLOWER TIP

The large, yellow, daisy-like flowers of C. grandiflora are ideal for cutting. It flowers profusely, providing a good supply of blooms all summer.

■ PLANTING TIP

Doronicum is the ideal plant if you have a shaded, cool border which rarely sees the sun. This plant thrives in cold, draughty places and is thus an excellent candidate for gloomy borders which it will cheer up in spring with its golden daisy-like flowers.

PERENNIALS

PAPAVER

| early summer | hardy | full sun | 60-90cm/2-3ft | 60cm/24in |

The oriental poppy, *Papaver orientale (above)*, is an eye-catching border plant bearing vivid but short-lived scarlet flowers up to 10cm/4 in across. Cultivated varieties extend the colour range to pink, crimson and white.

GROWING Set out young plants in small groups in autumn or early spring in free-draining soil in a sunny, open site sheltered from wind. Provide supporting canes for the growing plants. Cut back to ground level after flowering.

PROPAGATION Divide established plants in early spring and replant immediately. Alternatively, take root cuttings in winter and insert in a cold frame. Transfer to 7.5cm/3in pots of compost when 3 or 4 pairs of leaves have appeared. Stand outdoors in summer and set out in the autumn in the permanent site. Plants may also be raised from seed sown in spring in the greenhouse.

VARIETIES 'Black and White', white flowers, black centre; 'Perry's White'; 'King George', scarlet, frilled petals; 'Mrs Perry', soft coral; 'Enchantress', carmine.

POSSIBLE PROBLEMS Downy mildew on leaves.

VERBENA

| summer | half-hardy | full sun | 7.5-10cm/3-4in | 30cm/12in |

Verbena peruviana (above), a native of South America, is a low-growing perennial that looks best where its tiny though startlingly bright red flowers can spill over a sunny wall. It does well in a sheltered rock garden or a stone trough in a favoured corner. There are no named varieties of the species.

GROWING Light, free-draining, reasonably fertile soil is best. Give verbenas a sunny open site protected from wind. Pinch out growing tips of young plants to encourage sturdy, branching growth. Remove faded flowerheads regularly. Protect with cloches over winter.

PROPAGATION Raise plants from seed sown in winter/early spring in a greenhouse or propagator at 20-25°C/68-77°F. Prick the seedlings off into boxes when they are large enough to handle. Harden off before planting out in late spring/early summer.

POSSIBLE PROBLEMS Aphids may damage young shoots.

DRIED FLOWER TIP

The seed heads of poppies are widely used in dried flower arrangements. In a good year the seed heads can be allowed to dry out on the plant, or you can pick them and hang them up to dry in a loose bunch – no need to avoid sunlight in this case. Avoid picking flowers when they are wet or covered with dew.

ORGANIC TIP

Another plant that is a must in the organic garden, as its flowers are a good source of nectar, thus attracting bees and other nectar-feeding insects. Its sweet-smelling flowers are ideal if you want to create a scented border. Remember to dead-head regularly to keep it flowering.

TROPAEOLUM

| summer | hardy | shade | 3m/10ft | 90cm /3ft |

Tropaeolums include the familiar garden nasturtium, *T. majus*, and the canary creeper, *T. peregrinum*, both annuals, which climb by twisting their leaf stalks around any available support. *T. speciosum* (*above*), or flame nasturtium, is a rhizomatous perennial which bears bright red flowers on slender stems from mid to late summer. Attractive green leaves echo the radiating form of the petals. There are no named varieties of the species.

GROWING Despite its South American origin, the flame nasturtium does not like full sun – a shaded wall is ideal. Set out plants in spring in fertile, slightly acid soil, if necessary adding peat. Supports are essential, but a leafy shrub will serve this purpose as well as wires or canes.

PROPAGATION Divide the rhizomes in spring.

POSSIBLE PROBLEMS Aphids may infest the stems.

POTENTILLA

| summer | hardy | full sun | 30cm/12in | 45cm/18in |

Potentillas, commonly known as cinquefoil, were a favourite in sixteenth-century England and still claim a place in many modern gardeners' affections. *P. atrosanguinea* is a perennial species which is the parent to many garden hybrids. All are characterized by strawberry-like, grey-green leaves and sprays of five-petalled flowers like small wild roses. They are very long-lived plants and merit a prime spot in the border.

GROWING Set out young plants from autumn to spring in well-drained soil in full sun. Water generously in dry weather and apply an annual mulch of well-rotted manure in spring.

PROPAGATION Divide established plants in autumn or spring and replant immediately.

VARIETIES Choose from the hybrids 'Gibson's Scarlet' (*above*), semi-prostrate, useful for ground cover, single flowers; 'Yellow Queen', pure yellow, semi-double blooms, early flowering; 'Glory of Nancy', semi-double, crimson flowers; 'Wm Rollison', semi-double, bright orange flowers.

POSSIBLE PROBLEMS Generally trouble-free.

▨ PLANTING TIP

To minimize attack by aphids, plant alongside tagetes. These will attract hoverflies which feed on the nectar and the larvae of which will eat aphids.

▨ ORGANIC TIP

The marsh cinquefoil P. palustris is ideal if you are creating a wetland area in your garden. It will also thrive in any damp shady corner under trees.

POLYANTHUS

| spring | hardy | sun/semi-shade | 15-20cm/6-8in | 15-20cm/6-8in |

The primula family comprises a number of hardy perennials including *Primula veris*, the cowslip, and *P. vulgaris*, the primrose. The polyanthus is a hybrid of these two, with characteristic whorls of primrose flowers in a huge variety of colours, carried on strong stems above a rosette of oval leaves. They can be treated as indoor pot plants, but are ideal at the front of the border or in tubs and window boxes.

GROWING Set out plants in autumn or spring in heavy, moist soil into which plenty of organic matter has been incorporated. A site in full sun or partial shade will do.

PROPAGATION Divide the plants every 3 years immediately after flowering and replant straight away.

VARIETIES Pacific strain (*above*), large blooms, early flowering, bright colours including white, yellow, pink, red, purple and blue; 'Cowichan', mixed colours, no central eye.

POSSIBLE PROBLEMS Slugs on leaves in spring; grey mould; leaf spot on older plants.

LUPIN

| summer | hardy | sun | 90cm/3ft | 60cm/24in |

Lupins are traditionally a feature of informal cottage gardens, but their tall spires in a range of soft colours make a striking contribution to the border in any garden design. The most reliable types are hybrids of the species *L. polyphyllus*.

GROWING Set out young plants in early spring or in the autumn, in light, slightly acid soil. Neutral soils will do, but lupins hate lime, and in heavy soils the stems become too soft to support the flowers. Stake with twiggy sticks when plants are 15cm/6in high. Wait until late winter before cutting back, to prevent water lodging in the hollow stems.

PROPAGATION Take 7.5cm/3in cuttings, with a little rootstock attached, in spring. Insert in sandy soil in a cold frame; pot on when rooted or set in nursery rows before planting out in the autumn. Named varieties do not come true from seed.

VARIETIES Choose forms of the Russell lupin strain. Many are bi-coloured. 'Blushing Bride', cream and white; 'Cherry Pie', crimson and yellow; 'Jane Eyre', violet and white; 'Lilac Time', rose-lilac and white; 'Limelight', butter yellow; 'Guardsman', vermilion.

POSSIBLE PROBLEMS Crown rot, root rot, honey fungus.

ORGANIC TIP

To protect plants from slugs, sink a yoghurt pot into the ground nearby and fill with beer. The slugs are attracted to the liquid then fall in and drown.

SPECIAL CARE TIP

Lupins seed themselves very easily, so if you don't want lupins all over the garden the seed heads should be removed in good time. Remove the tips of the flower spikes before the seeds have time to form – it will also ensure that the plant keeps on flowering.

IMPATIENS

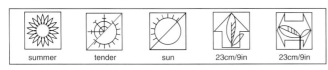

| summer | tender | sun | 23cm/9in | 23cm/9in |

Familiar even to non-gardeners, *Impatiens walleriana* or busy lizzie is a short-lived perennial native to Africa. Usually grown indoors or in a greenhouse, dwarf hybrids between *I. walleriana* and *I. sultanii* can be used in outdoor bedding schemes and are ideal for tubs and windowboxes. They are admired for their dense foliage and five-petalled flowers of red, pink or white which appear throughout the summer.

GROWING Set young plants out in early summer in well-drained soil in a sheltered position. Pinch out the growing tips to promote bushy growth. Dead-head regularly.

PROPAGATION Sow seed in pans in spring at 16-18°C/61-64°F. Prick the seedlings off into boxes when they are large enough to handle, then into individual 7.5cm/3in pots of compost. Harden off before planting out.

VARIETIES The Imp strain (*above*) includes varieties in white, shocking pink, carmine, scarlet and purple; 'Tangleglow', orange; 'Zig Zag', striped.

POSSIBLE PROBLEMS Aphids infest leaves and stems. Slugs may damage seedlings.

BELLIS

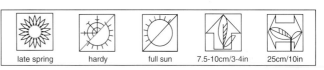

| late spring | hardy | full sun | 7.5-10cm/3-4in | 25cm/10in |

The perennial daisy, *Bellis perennis*, is a charming if short-lived plant for the front of the border or as attractive ground cover. Unlike the simple daisy of the meadows, flowers are large, the foliage glossy and almost evergreen, and the colour range includes pink, red and white as well as bi-coloured forms.

GROWING Treat as biennials. Set out young plants in autumn in any ordinary garden soil. Daisies prefer sun but do reasonably well in partial shade. Dead-head regularly – though daisies will self-seed, the resulting seedlings are poor. Discard or divide plants after flowering.

PROPAGATION Divide named varieties immediately after flowering. Sow seeds in boxes or in the open in late spring and grow on in a nursery bed before planting out in autumn for flowering the following spring.

VARIETIES Monstrosa forms include double-flowered varieties such as 'Giant Double', mixed or single colours. Double miniature varieties have tiny pompon flowers; try 'Pomponette' (*above*); 'Dresden China', pink; 'Quilled Mixed'; 'Rob Roy', red; 'Victoria', red and white.

POSSIBLE PROBLEMS Generally trouble-free.

▨ PROPAGATION TIP

To propagate by taking cuttings: in spring, make a clean cut from new shoots of plants which have over-wintered indoors or in a heated greenhouse.

▨ PLANTING TIP

One of the more traditional plants used in raised flowerbeds. To make a raised bed, cut a geometric shape in the turf. The soil is slightly heaped up, rising towards the centre so that the flowerbed is about 40cm/16in higher than the rest of the garden. Plant out in autumn for spring flowers.

HELLEBORUS

winter	hardy	semi-shade	30-45cm /12-18in	45cm/18in

No gardener who wants to enjoy flowers all the year round can afford to ignore the Christmas rose, *Helleborus niger*, which produces its exquisite white blooms in deepest winter. The Lenten rose, *H. orientalis*, is equally valuable, blooming from winter into early spring with dramatically coloured flowers of green, white, pink, red-purple or black-purple, often splashed inside with a contrasting colour. As cut flowers hellebores are very long-lasting.

GROWING Set out young plants in small groups in autumn in deep, moisture-retentive but well-drained soil into which plenty of well-rotted compost or leaf mould has been incorporated. Choose a site where they can be left for years: they dislike disturbance. Protect the flowers of the Christmas rose as they open with cloches. Cut stems right back after flowering; apply an annual mulch in the autumn.

PROPAGATION Divide well-established plants in spring and replant immediately. Alternatively sow seeds in sandy soil in a cold frame in summer. Prick off the seedlings into a nursery bed and grow on until planting out in the autumn of the following year. They will not flower for 2-3 years.

VARIETIES *H. niger* 'Potter's Wheel' (*above*), exceptional white form.

POSSIBLE PROBLEMS Leaf spot.

ALTHAEA

summer	hardy	semi-shade	2.4m/8ft	90cm/3ft

Althaea rosea (above), the familiar hollyhock, is well suited to cottage gardens and because of its great height looks impressive at the back of an informal border, particularly when a fine old wall provides protection. The showy, trumpet-shaped flowers of the species are in shades of pink, but named varieties are available in red, cream and white.

GROWING Hollyhocks do best if treated as biennials. Set out young plants in autumn in any ordinary soil, in a sheltered site. Strong stakes should be provided from early spring. On light soils, apply a moisture-retaining mulch in hot weather. For perennial growth, cut back plants after flowering to 15cm/6in; otherwise discard the plants.

PROPAGATION Sow seed in trays of compost in early spring. Prick the seedlings out into 7.5cm/3in pots when they are large enough to handle and plant out in late summer for flowering the following year.

VARIETIES 'Chater's Double', peony-like double flowers, all colours; 'Begonia Flowered Crested', mixed colours.

POSSIBLE PROBLEMS Caterpillars damage the stems and leaves. Rust is more likely on plants treated as perennials and can be severe.

▮ PLANTING TIP

If using a container-grown plant, ensure that the root ball gets enough moisture when first planted. Dig a hole that is big enough for the roots, sprinkle a general fertilizer around the rim and firm in. 'Puddle in' the plant by giving enough water so that a puddle forms. Avoid moving hellebores once sited.

▮ ORGANIC TIP

Rust occurs when growing conditions are poor. Instead of using chemical sprays, make sure the soil is fed properly with manure or compost before planting.

CONVALLARIA

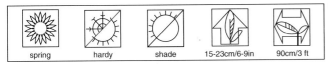

| spring | hardy | shade | 15-23cm/6-9in | 90cm/3 ft |

The lily-of-the-valley, *Convallaria majalis (above)*, is one of the prettiest spring flowers, its graceful stems clothed with pure white bell-shaped blooms. With handsome leaves, it makes excellent ground cover in shady spots, spreading by means of creeping rhizomes. The lightly fragrant flowers are popular with flower arrangers.

GROWING Start with 'pips' (root pieces with buds). Plant in autumn 5cm/2in deep in heavy, moisture-retentive soil that has previously been enriched with plenty of well-rotted organic matter. Mulch with leaf mould every autumn.

PROPAGATION Lift the rhizomes between autumn and spring and separate into crowns; replant, just covering with soil, and dress with leaf mould. Water well.

VARIETIES 'Fortin's Giant', white; 'Rosea', pink; 'Variegata', leaves striped with gold.

POSSIBLE PROBLEMS Caterpillars damage the rhizomes; grey mould on leaves in wet weather.

TIARELLA

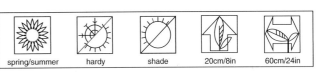

| spring/summer | hardy | shade | 20cm/8in | 60cm/24in |

The foam flower, *Tiarella cordifolia (above)*, like lily-of-the-valley *(left)* is a good subject for cool shady places, where it will spread out to smother weeds with its soft green pointed leaves. Foliage is retained throughout the winter. Spikes of tiny, very pale pink flowers appear in early summer. No named varieties of this species are available. *T. wherryi* is similar but slow-growing, with attractive autumn foliage.

GROWING Set out young plants in autumn or spring in moist, rich, well-drained soil. Water in dry weather to maintain growth and apply an annual mulch of leaf mould or peat in spring.

PROPAGATION Divide established plants of foam flower in autumn or spring and replant rooted pieces immediately. *T. wherryi* does not divide easily.

POSSIBLE PROBLEMS Generally trouble-free.

▪ PLANTING TIP

One of the essential plants when creating a scented border. Make sure you choose a shady spot near the house so the scent can waft in on summer nights.

▪ ORGANIC TIP

Nature's answer to the problem of weed control are the perennial ground-cover plants which in time will spread out to smother most troublesome weeds.

Tiarella is a perfect example – low-growing with nice leaves, it is the organic solution to the weed problem being dense enough to kill off all competitors.

PELARGONIUM

| summer | tender | sun | 30-60cm/12-24in | 20cm/8in |

Pelargoniums are often (wrongly) called geraniums, the name properly given to the hardy perennial cranesbill (*see p. 56*). Native to Africa, these tender species with their showy blooms are an essential element in hanging baskets, window boxes and tubs as well as summer bedding schemes. Among the most popular types for this purpose are the hybrids known as Regal and Zonal pelargoniums, which are available in all shades of pink, red, maroon and white. Zonal hybrids have beautifully coloured leaves.

GROWING Set out young plants in early summer in moderately fertile soil in full sun. Remove faded flowerheads. Water freely, giving a high-potash feed occasionally. In autumn put plants under protection. Cut back older plants and put up in good compost.

PROPAGATION Take cuttings from overwintered plants in spring and insert in a peat/sand mixture. Pot on when rooted. Plants may also be raised successfully from seed sown under protection in early spring.

VARIETIES 'Princess of Wales', frilled, strawberry pink; 'Grand Slam' (*above*), abundant rose-red blooms; 'Nomad', white, blotched pink. Many other good varieties.

POSSIBLE PROBLEMS Low night temperatures cause reddening of leaves and stems. Leaves turn yellow if soil is too dry.

MALVA

| summer | hardy | sun/semi-shade | 1.2m/4ft | 45-60cm/18-24in |

The mallow, *Malva alcea*, is a tall, bushy plant particularly useful on poor soils. It bears abundant mauve trumpet-shaped flowers all summer.

GROWING Plant from autumn to spring on light, well-drained soil in sun or partial shade. Provide twiggy sticks for support. Cut down dead stems in late autumn or winter.

PROPAGATION Take 7.5cm/3in basal cuttings in late spring. Insert in sandy soil in a cold frame and transfer to the flowering site in autumn. Plants may be raised from seed sown under protection with gentle warmth in spring. Prick the seedlings out into a nursery bed when they are large enough to handle and grow on until transferring to the flowering site in the autumn.

VARIETIES *M. alcea* 'Fastigiata' (*above*) is more upright than the species and reaches only 90cm/3ft.

POSSIBLE PROBLEMS Rust may affect the leaves and stems.

▓ PLANTING TIP

Pelargoniums are the perfect flowers – ideal for a host of situations and almost trouble-free. Whatever your needs, there are types to suit: regal pelargoniums for bedding or massed border display schemes, trailing ivy-leaved ones for hanging baskets and zonal foliage ones for window-boxes and tubs.

▓ ORGANIC TIP

Rust is often a symptom of poor soils. If it is a real problem, try mulching the soil with well-rotted compost or provide a feed of liquid seaweed.

STOKESIA

| summer | hardy | sun/semi-shade | 30-45cm/12-18in | 45cm/18in |

Stokesia laevis is a wonderfully rewarding plant. It bears corn-flower-like blooms of blue, lavender or creamy-white that are 10cm/4in across and continue right through the summer. Its long-lasting foliage and spreading habit contribute useful ground cover.

GROWING Set out young plants in spring in sun or partial shade in light, well-drained soil. Shelter from cold winds is appreciated and the plants should be staked with light twigs in early summer.

PROPAGATION Divide established plants in spring and replant without delay.

VARIETIES 'Blue Star', light blue flowers, 7.5cm/3in across; 'Silver Moon', white with lilac centre; 'Cyanea' (*above*), lavender.

POSSIBLE PROBLEMS Generally trouble-free.

ASTILBE

| summer | hardy | shade | 45cm-1.2m/18in-4ft | 60-90cm/2-3ft |

Astilbe species come from China and Japan. From these the garden hybrid *A. × arendsii* (*above*) has been developed to display the best qualities of the family. They are bushy, erect plants, forming impressive clumps of fern-like leaves; the taller types are most effective for ground cover. Feathery plumes of pink or white flowers are carried on delicate stems. They make excellent waterside plants.

GROWING Plant from autumn to spring in moist soil in a cool, shady position (although a sunny site is acceptable if the soil is never allowed to dry out). Astilbes dislike chalky soil. Water well in dry weather and apply an annual moisture-retaining mulch such as leaf mould, well-rotted compost or manure in early spring. Do not cut the plants back until the end of winter, as the faded flowerheads and foliage are attractive in their own right.

PROPAGATION Divide woody clumps in spring, ensuring that each portion has 2-3 developing buds.

VARIETIES 'Fanal', 60cm/24in, red; 'Bressingham Beauty', 90cm/3ft, rose-pink; 'Deutschland', 60cm/24in, brilliant white.

POSSIBLE PROBLEMS Generally trouble-free.

■ SPECIAL CARE TIP

This attractive perennial is quite easy to grow, but it must have a well-drained soil – on heavy, wet or clay soils it will be very short-lived. If necessary, there-fore, improve drainage before planting by digging deep, and incorporating one or two bucketfuls of gravel and organic material into the soil.

■ PLANTING TIP

This tall, bushy plant is ideal for the centre or back of the border. As with most perennials, remember to give it enough 'elbow room' to allow for future growth.

PULMONARIA

spring	hardy	shade	30cm/12in	45cm/18in

Pulmonarias are ideal plants for a shady part of the garden, where they will spread their handsome oval leaves to make dense ground cover. In early spring clusters of drooping bell-shaped flowers appear, held clear of the foliage on erect stems. The blooms are pink, often turning blue later.

GROWING Set out young plants in autumn or spring in reasonably moist fertile soil. Apply an annual mulch of peat in spring and water well during the growing period. Remove dead leaves in the autumn.

PROPAGATION Divide established clumps in autumn or spring.

SPECIES *P. angustifolia* (blue cowslip), height 23cm/9in, dark green leaves, spring-flowering; *P. officinalis* (Jerusalem cowslip), height 23-30cm/9-12in, light green leaves blotched silver, late spring-flowering; *P. saccharata* (*above*), 30cm/12in, pointed leaves beautifully marked cream, late spring-flowering; the variety 'White Wings' bears white flowers.

POSSIBLE PROBLEMS Slugs may eat young shoots.

ASTRANTIA

summer	hardy	semi-shade	60cm/24in	45cm/18in

Native to Europe and Western Asia, this group of herbaceous perennials includes three species which are well suited to summer borders or informal planting schemes. All have attractive divided leaves and bear tiny but numerous white or pale pink star-shaped flowers. They last well as cut flowers.

GROWING Set out young plants between autumn and spring in well-drained, fertile soil. Semi-shade is best but full sun is tolerated, as long as the soil does not dry out. Apply a moisture-conserving mulch in spring. Cut plants back to ground level in late autumn.

PROPAGATION Divide roots in autumn or spring

SPECIES *A. major* (*above*), fresh green leaves, pinkish-green flowers surrounded by silver bracts; *A. maxima*, similar to *A. major* but bolder in effect, with pink bracts; *A. carniolica*, mid-green, slender leaves, white flowers – the variety 'Rubra' is only 30cm/12in high with deep crimson flowers and bracts.

POSSIBLE PROBLEMS Generally trouble-free.

■ ORGANIC TIP

With attractively marked leaves and clusters of drooping bell-flowers, this is the perfect answer if you need weed control or ground cover for shady parts of the garden, such as under trees and shrubs, or in the shade of hedges. Brighten up dark corners with the 'Argentea' variety which has white flowers.

■ CUT FLOWER TIP

An old favourite, grown for hundreds of years, and very highly regarded as a cut flower because the unusual star-shaped blooms last well. Suitable for drying.

CATANANCHE

summer	hardy	sun	45cm/18in	38cm/15in

Catananche caerulea or cupid's dart bears blue cornflower-like flowers throughout the summer. It is a good plant for the border or for cut flowers, and can be dried very successfully for winter decoration.

GROWING Set out young plants from early autumn to late spring in light, well-drained soil. On exposed sites it may be advisable to support the plants with pea-sticks. Cut down the dead stems in autumn.

PROPAGATION Catananches are short-lived perennials. Take root cuttings in the spring of their third or fourth year to be sure of continuing stock. Insert 7.5cm/3in cuttings in seed compost in a cold frame and transplant to a nursery bed when the leaves are well formed. Transfer to the permanent position in the autumn or following spring.

VARIETIES 'Major' (*above*), large, lavender-blue flowers; 'Perry's White'; 'Bicolor', white with blue eyes.

POSSIBLE PROBLEMS Generally trouble-free.

BERGENIA

spring	hardy	sun/semi-shade	30-45cm/12-18in	60cm/24in

Bergenias are among the elite of evergreen ground cover plants, with large, glossy, handsome leaves and nodding clusters of bell-shaped flowers. Both foliage and flowers are prized by flower arrangers, too.

GROWING Almost any situation will do, as long as the soil is reasonably moist and fertile. The best winter leaf colour will be achieved on open sites. Plant in autumn or spring and leave undisturbed until the clump is overcrowded. Pick off damaged leaves and remove flower stems after flowering.

PROPAGATION Lift and divide established plants in the autumn. Select single-rooted portions and replant immediately.

VARIETIES Choose from hybrids such as 'Abendglut' (syn. 'Evening Glow', *above*), deep magenta flowers, leaves reddish-bronze in favourable conditions; 'Morgenrot' (syn. Morning Blush'), pink, often flowers twice, in spring and summer.

POSSIBLE PROBLEMS Leaf spot may discolour the leaves.

▦ DRIED FLOWER TIP

To dry the beautiful blooms of these plants, tie them in small bunches and hang upside down in a dark shed or attic (darkness prevents the colours fading).

▦ PLANTING TIP

This attractive plant will grow almost anywhere, in sun or shade, but you have to make a choice – grow in the open for best winter leaf colour, or in a sheltered spot, free from spring flowers for the best show of flowers.

BRUNNERA

| spring | hardy | shade | 45cm/18in | 60cm/24in |

Brunnera macrophylla, sometimes listed as *Anchusa myosotid-iflora*, is related to the forget-me-not, as can easily be seen from its airy clusters of tiny blue flowers. It is a quick-growing plant with large, heart-shaped leaves that make attractive ground cover for shade and under trees. The leaves of variegated forms are splashed cream or silver.

GROWING Set out young plants between autumn and spring in any type of fertile soil, even chalk. Do not let the soil dry out. Variegated forms need a cool, sheltered position. Remove old stems after flowering and cut the plant down to ground level in late autumn.

PROPAGATION Divide and replant the roots in autumn or spring.

VARIETIES The species is vigorous and reliable. Interesting forms are 'Variegata', with leaves splashed creamy-white, and 'Langtrees', with silvery-grey markings on the leaves.

POSSIBLE PROBLEMS Generally trouble-free.

CAMPANULA

| summer | hardy | sun | 30-90cm/1-3ft | 30-38cm/12-15in |

The bellflower family includes a great number of attractive species including *Campanula medium*, the well-loved biennial Canterbury bell, and several exquisite alpine plants. For the border, *C. persicifolia*, the peach-leaved campanula, is an excellent choice with its impressive height, breathtaking flowers and evergreen foliage. *C. Lactiflora* (*above*) bears pale, lavender-blue, bell-shaped flowers in early and mid summer.

GROWING Set out young plants in autumn in well-drained fertile soil; chalky soils are tolerated. A sunny site is preferred but light shade will do no great harm. Stake the plants when they reach 15cm/6in high.

PROPAGATION Divide established clumps in autumn. *C. persicifolia* does not come true from seed.

VARIETIES *C. persicifolia* 'Telham Beauty', deep, rich blue; 'Planiflora' (syn. *C. nitida*), dwarf at 23-30cm/9-12in, blue flowers; 'Planiflora Alba' is a white form.

POSSIBLE PROBLEMS Slugs and snails may damage leaves and shoots. Leaf spot fungus and rust may damage leaves.

▦ PLANTING TIP

Enrich the soil with manure or well-rotted leaf mould before planting. Mulch with manure or well-rotted compost in the spring to help conserve moisture.

▦ PLANTING TIP

The best-known, and most popular, variety is probably the tall Canterbury bell, which needs lots of room. But even if space is a problem, it is still possible to enjoy this beautiful plant. C. Cochleavifolia is ideal for a wall or rock garden where it forms low mats of leaves with dainty bell-shaped flowers.

DELPHINIUM

| summer | hardy | sun | 90cm-1.5m/3-5ft | 45-60cm/18-24in |

Delphiniums are unquestionably the most magnificent flowers in the herbaceous border. Quite apart from their great height, the profusion of blooms and intensity of colour – usually blue, but sometimes pink or cream – make an unforgettable impression. Most garden types are hybrids bred from *D. elatum* and other species, giving two strains known as Elatum or Large-flowered (up to 2.4m/8ft, and including the Pacific hybrids, *above*) and Belladonna (about 1.2m/4ft).

GROWING Set out young plants from autumn to spring in deep, rich soil on a sheltered site. Provide stout canes for support. Cut back to ground level after flowering.

PROPAGATION Divide established plants in spring or take 7.5cm/3in basal cuttings and insert in a peat/sand mixture in a cold frame. Transfer to a nursery bed when rooted and grow on until planting out in autumn.

VARIETIES The choice is wide. 'Blue Jade', Pacific, dwarf at 1.2m/4ft, sky-blue; 'Wendy', Belladonna, gentian blue; 'Butterball', Elatum, rich cream.

POSSIBLE PROBLEMS Slugs and snails damage young shoots.

ECHINOPS

| summer | hardy | sun | 1.2m/4ft | 60cm/24in |

The globe thistle, *Echinops banaticus* (*above*) is a valuable addition to the border, with dramatic dark green foliage and round, steel-blue flowerheads held high. The flowers are prized for winter decoration when dried. No named varieties of the species are available.

GROWING Set out young plants from autumn to spring in deep, well-drained soil; echinops do well on chalk. A sunny, sheltered position is best. It may be necessary to provide stakes for support on exposed sites, but usually this is not required. Mulch lightly in spring, and cut the stems down in the autumn.

PROPAGATION Divide established plants between autumn and spring.

POSSIBLE PROBLEMS Generally trouble-free.

▮ SPECIAL CARE TIP

Delphiniums are not difficult to grow, provided the young plants are well looked after. If necessary, make sure there is shelter from strong winds and provide staking early enough. Protect from slugs, otherwise the young plants can disappear overnight. Try 'slug pubs' (see p 92) or organic powders.

▮ DRIED FLOWER TIP

The blue flowerheads are popular for arrangements. To dry the flowers, cut the heads before fully opened and hang upside down in a dark, airy place.

GERANIUM

summer	hardy	sun	23cm/9in	90cm/3ft

Geraniums, popularly known as cranesbills, comprise a large family of flowering plants, including some alpine species. All summer and into the autumn, they bear open, five-petalled flowers about 25cm/1in or more across, in shades of pink, crimson, blue and white. The leaves are rounded, sometimes deeply cut; the plants form large round clumps that look attractive in the summer border or any informal planting scheme.

GROWING Set out young plants between autumn and spring in any type of well-drained soil. Do not let them dry out in hot weather.

PROPAGATION Divide and replant established clumps in autumn or spring.

SPECIES *G. endressii* reaches 40cm/16in in height and spreads to 60cm/24in or more. Named varieties include 'A.T. Johnson', silvery pink, and 'Rose Clair', white edged purple. The hybrid G. × 'Claridge Druce', with deep mauve blooms, makes excellent ground cover. *G. sanguineum* (*above*) is low-growing, matforming, with magenta flowers; *G. s. lancastrense* is a great favourite with pale pink flowers veined with red.

POSSIBLE PROBLEMS Slugs may eat young plants.

VIOLA

all year	hardy	sun/semi-shade	23cm/9in	23cm/9in

Garden pansies, *Viola × wittrockiana*, are short-lived perennial hybrids. They are among the most popular of all cultivated plants, with their large, colourful flowers, bushy foliage and easy-going nature. The colour range is huge and different varieties are in bloom almost all year.

GROWING Time of planting depends on variety. Set out in moisture-retentive but well-drained soil. Add peat and/or leaf mould to chalky soils. Snip off faded flowers to ensure a succession of blooms.

PROPAGATION Divide mature plants in early spring or take 5cm/2in cuttings of non-flowering basal shoots in summer and insert in a peat/sand mixture in a cold frame. Pot on when rooted and plant out in autumn or spring.

VARIETIES Countless varieties are available, in single colours – white, yellow, apricot, red, violet and blue – and numerous combinations, often with a black blotch.

POSSIBLE PROBLEMS Leaf spot; fungi of different kinds cause pansy sickness.

▓ ORGANIC TIP

Geranium is also known as meadow cranesbill, and at one time was a common wild flower found in open meadows. It attracts bees and other insects, and the birds will feed on its seeds. It is an ideal flower to grow if you want to create a natural-looking flowery meadow at the end of your garden.

▓ PLANTING TIP

A highly versatile plant which can be used to edge borders or paths, in rock gardens, in window-boxes and containers and as ground cover under trees.

AQUILEGIA

| summer | hardy | sun | 60-90cm/2-3ft | 30-45cm/12-18in |

A number of very beautiful hybrids have been raised from *Aquilegia vulgaris*, the columbine or, to give it its old country name, granny's bonnet. The plants are characterized by pretty fern-like leaves and graceful funnel-shaped flowers with a spur behind each petal. They are very effective in the border and in cottage garden schemes. Blooms may be single or bi-coloured in pink, blue, cream, green, yellow or red.

GROWING Set out young plants in autumn in fertile, well-drained soil. An open, sunny site is best but light shade is tolerated. Do not let them dry out. Mulch in early spring to conserve moisture. Unless seed is required, dead-head and cut the stems (not the leaves) to ground level after flowering.

PROPAGATION Divide established clumps into single-rooted pieces from autumn to spring. Columbines produce seed freely. Allow the plants to self-seed or collect the seed when ripe and sow in nursery beds in spring, transplanting to the permanent site in autumn.

VARIETIES 'McKana Hybrids', large flowers, many colours, 90cm/3ft high.

POSSIBLE PROBLEMS Aphids; leaf spot.

MONARDA

| summer | hardy | sun/semi-shade | 60cm/24in | 38cm/15in |

Bees and butterflies are irresistibly attracted to the vivid, shaggy flowers of *Monarda didyma*, a highly decorative relative of mint which is variously known as bee balm or Oswego tea. Native to North America, it was used by the Oswego Indians to make a soothing drink – the leaves have a minty fragrance. It is named after Nicolas Monardes, author of a sixteenth-century herbal first published in America. Quick-growing and perfect for cutting, Monarda is a good choice for the middle of the border.

GROWING Plant in groups of 4-6 in spring or autumn in moisture-retentive soil. Mulch annually in spring with well-rotted organic matter. A position in sun or partial shade will do. Cut down the stems in autumn.

PROPAGATION Monarda spreads from the roots. Divide established clumps every 3 years. Discard the centre and replant small outer tufts. Named varieties do not come true from seed.

VARIETIES 'Cambridge Scarlet', bright red; 'Croftway Pink', shell pink; 'Snow Maiden', white; 'Prairie Night', indigo-purple.

POSSIBLE PROBLEMS Generally trouble-free.

◾ ORGANIC TIP

Practise companion planting – plant tagetes and other insect-attracting flowers beside it in the border. The larvae of hoverflies eat aphids.

◾ ORGANIC TIP

One of the perfect plants for the organic garden as its scarlet, shaggy flowers attract butterflies and bees. To make the soothing drink of the Oswego Indians, steep 1 teaspoon of monarda leaves in a cup of hot water.

CALTHA

spring	hardy	sun/semi-shade	30-38cm/12-15in	23-30cm/9-12in

Caltha palustris, the kingcup or marsh marigold, will grow in water up to 15 cm/6in deep, but is happiest with the crown just submerged or at the water's edge. It produces a brilliant display of spring blooms up to 5 cm/2 in across. The glossy green leaves form rounded hummocks.

GROWING Plant in spring, in sun or partial shade. If in water, plants should be in containers or aquatic baskets. Use heavy soil, with a layer of shingle on top to prevent it muddying the water. In the garden, the best soil for calthas is heavy, moisture-retentive loam, preferably slightly acid. It must be kept constantly moist.

PROPAGATION Divide in early spring, when the young shoots appear.

VARIETIES 'Alba', white 'petals' (actually sepals), prominent yellow stamens; 'Plena' (*above*), low-growing, double flowers, green at first opening to rich golden yellow.

POSSIBLE PROBLEMS Rust on leaves caused by fungi.

PAEONIA

spring/summer	hardy	sun/semi-shade	60-90cm/2-3ft	45-60cm/18-24in

Peonies have an exotic air, with huge, bowl-shaped flowers that open in late spring or early summer. Large, handsome leaves set off to perfection the blooms of white, yellow, pink or red, some of which are double, some fragrant.

GROWING Peonies like moisture-retentive, well-drained soil, in sun or partial shade; choose a site that is sheltered from early morning sun. Before planting, dig the ground to a spade's depth, incorporating plenty of well-rotted organic matter. Set out young plants in suitable weather between autumn and spring, with the crowns just 2.5cm/1in below the soil surface. On light soil especially, mulch each spring with well-rotted compost. Peonies resent disturbance – choose a site where they can be left alone. Dead-head regularly. Cut back foliage in autumn.

PROPAGATION Divide and replant in early autumn, cutting the crowns with a sharp knife.

VARIETIES *Paeonia lactiflora* hybrids: 'Whitleyi Major', white, single flowers, golden stamens; 'The Moor', deep crimson, single; 'Felix Crousse', rose-red, double. *P. officinalis*: 'Alba Plena' (*above*): double, white; 'Rubra Plena', double, deep red.

POSSIBLE PROBLEMS Peony blight; leaf spot.

■ ORGANIC TIP

Ideal if you are creating a wildlife garden, or even a wetland area, as this plant enjoys wet or damp conditions on the edge of a pool, or any damp spot.

■ ORGANIC TIP

This is the ideal plant to benefit from your home-grown compost, well rotted down in a pit or container. Peonies don't like being moved, so prepare the site by digging plenty of compost before planting, to enrich the soil. Thereafter, mulch each spring with more compost or well-rotted manure.

HEMEROCALLIS

| summer | hardy | sun | 90cm/3ft | 45cm/18in |

Three species of the hemerocallis are available, but much more popular are hybrids which can be found in dozens of different colours. The common name, day lily, refers to the fact that each flower lives for one day only, to be replaced by another the next morning. This process continues for 6-8 weeks; by choosing a mixture of varieties it is possible to have a display of these fabulous blooms for the entire summer.

GROWING Plant between autumn and spring in moist, rich soil. Full sun is preferred but a little shade is tolerated. Remove dead stems and leaves in late autumn.

PROPAGATION Divide established clumps in early autumn or spring just as young growth starts. Seeds do not come true to type.

VARIETIES 'Golden Chimes' (*above*); 'Chartreuse Magic', sharp yellow and green; 'Morocco Red', dusky red and yellow; 'Pink Damask', pink with yellow throat.

POSSIBLE PROBLEMS Generally trouble-free.

TROLLIUS

| summer | hardy | sun | 60cm/24in | 45cm/18in |

There are several species of trollius, the globe flower, in cultivation, all bearing impressive rounded blooms in various shades of yellow with prominent stamens. They are ideal for waterside planting or in the border, coming into flower in late spring and again in late summer if the stems are cut right back after flowering.

GROWING Plant out in autumn or spring in rather heavy, moisture-retentive soil. Keep well-watered, especially in hot dry spells. Some shade is tolerated.

PROPAGATION Divide the fibrous rootstock in autumn and replant immediately.

SPECIES *Trollius ledebourii* (*above*), bright, orange-yellow, cup-shaped flowers; *T. × cultorum*, garden hybrid, only 30-45cm/12-18in high. Good varieties are 'Earliest of All', clear yellow; 'Salamander', reddish orange; 'Canary Bird', pale yellow.

POSSIBLE PROBLEMS Smut causes swellings on leaves and stems.

▓ PLANTING TIP

If you are short of space, and need an attractive display for a container or a tub, this is the answer. Tall and striking, these exotic flowers will prove a real eye-catcher if planted to stand tall among the trailing foliage of variegated ivy, or another trailer or ground-cover plant.

▓ PLANTING TIP

All parts of this plant are poisonous, so avoid planting it if you have young children who might be tempted to pick the attractive yellow flowers.

BULBS

Flowers grown from bulbs are inevitably associated with spring. The cheerful appearance of daffodils and crocuses announcing the start of a new year is a sight that raises everyone's spirits after the dull days of winter. There are, however, bulbs, corms and tubers for every season and indeed for every situation. It is this versatility that makes bulbs so valuable.

In botanical terms a bulb is a shoot, surrounded by tightly packed leaves arranged roughly in a sphere, with fine roots issuing from beneath. In some instances the leaves simply overlap each other; examples of these so-called scaly bulbs are lilies and fritillaries. In both cases these leaves are storage organs containing reserve food to nourish foliage and flowers. Corms, for example crocuses, gladiolus and colchicums, are storage organs composed of a thickened stem base; tubers, for example dahlias and begonias, are swollen underground branches with 'eyes' (buds) from which new plants are produced. Zantedeschias and some irises grow from rhi-

zomes, which are swollen underground stems from which a number of flowering stems arise. Bulbs are planted at different depths according to type. Most like sun or light shade and thrive in light, naturally rich soil. They should not be planted in contact with crude manure.

COLOUR THE YEAR ROUND Snowdrops (*Galanthus nivalis*) appear in the middle of winter, closely followed by the bright yellow flowers of the winter aconite (*Eranthis hyemalis*). Crocuses, scillas and chionodoxas enliven the cold bright days of very early spring, and then the glorious daffodil comes into its own. Daffodils – the genus *Narcissus* – have, like roses and chrysanthemums, attracted an enormous fan club, not only because of their individual beauty, but also their extraordinary variety. Most people are unaware of the range of narcissus (daffodils, strictly speaking, are narcissus whose central trumpet is as long as the surrounding petals). There are far too many individual species – about 60 – to describe here, but mention of three will demonstrate their diversity (and there are hundreds of hybrids as well). *N. bulbocodium*, at most 15cm/ 6in high, is unique, with leaves like chives. Very long, curved stamens protrude from 2.5cm/1in trumpets that open wide, almost concealing the tiny petals. The poet's narcissus, *N. poeticus*, reaches 45cm/18in with white petals but bright red, frilly cups. An old favourite is the hybrid *N. × odorus* (campernelle jonquil), 45cm/18in high, with 2-3 large, scented flowers to each stem. From this the richly scented, brightly coloured form 'Sweetness' has been developed.

Muscari, scilla, hyacinth and leucojum bring flourishes of blue, white, yellow and pink to the spring garden. For adding oranges and reds to the picture (as well as subtle hues of pink, yellow and cream), tulips cannot be bettered. Like daffodils, they have their devoted followers and display a dazzling variety of forms.

Blue, purple, yellow and white, irises bloom from late spring into summer. And in summer the colour range is stretched to the limit when gladioli and lilies come into

bloom. These beautiful flowers are much used for indoor decoration but because of their height and erect habit must placed with care in the border. Lilies look splendid grouped together, rather than trying to integrate them, perhaps with a low-growing plant with decorative leaves at their feet. Clumps of the shorter gladiolus hybrids can be set in the middle of a mixed border, especially if offset with the interesting foliage of *Alchemilla mollis* or *Euphorbia robbiae*.

A garden with dahlias will never lack for autumn colour. These beautiful flowers come in a range of gorgeous colours and in a number of different forms, from neat pompons to the open anemone-flowered types. They bloom freely until the first frosts. Colchicums (autumn crocus) provide a subtler alternative for informal and cottage gardens. After they have faded, it is a matter of weeks before snowdrops reappear and the cycle begins again.

BULBS IN CONTAINERS Because of their varying sizes and flowering times, bulbs can be used in almost any part of the garden. They are also excellent for tubs, window-boxes and troughs. Miniature species are particularly well suited to containers which can be set at a level where tiny plants, which would be overlooked in the border, can be appreciated. An alpine garden in a trough could include the very early-

A display of zantedeschias provides the focal point of this cool green and white garden, the low box hedges providing a perfect foil for the tall, pointed leaves.

flowering *Iris histrioides* or *Narcissus juncifolius*. Some of the most brilliant effects are achieved by planting numbers of a single species in one container, so that they all flower at the same time. In fact, bulbs look best set in groups whatever the situation. Dwarf tulips with interesting foliage look marvellous in stone troughs or half-barrels. Try *T. clusiana*, the lady tulip, with narrow grey-green leaves and white flowers flushed red, or *T. greigii*, whose grey-green leaves are marbled purple and brown, the flowers vivid red.

LIFTING BULBS Some bulbs, such as gladiolus, are not hardy enough to withstand the winter in very cold areas, and must be lifted and stored. In formal bedding schemes bulbs are lifted when they are past their best in order to make way for the next feature, and when bulbs are congested they can be lifted, their offsets detached, and replanted at greater distances. Generally, however, bulbs can be left undisturbed for many years, another characteristic that endears them to modern gardeners with little time to spare for demanding planting schemes.

CROCUS

spring	hardy	full sun	7.5cm/3in	7.5cm/3in

The sight of budding crocuses is welcomed as a signal of spring. In fact these hardy plants, grown from corms, flower from late summer until spring, according to species. Colours include blue, purple, white, yellow and mauve. Some varieties are striped; many have vivid golden stamens. Very low-growing, with cup-shaped flowers rising directly from the ground, crocuses do well in rock gardens, troughs and at the edge of a border. Winter and early spring-flowering types can be used in lawns.

GROWING Plant in autumn in well-drained soil, preferably in groups, in a sunny position with protection from wind. Do not dead-head; leave the foliage until it is yellow and can be pulled off easily.

PROPAGATION Take offsets after flowering. Replant the larger cormlets for flowering the following year. The smaller ones can be grown on in drills until they reach flowering size.

SPECIES Try hybrids of *Crocus chrysanthus* such as 'E. P. Bowles', butter yellow, spring-flowering; *C. longiflorus* is scented, autumn-flowering, deep purple; spring-flowering Dutch crocuses deriving from *C. vernus* include 'Joan of Arc', white and 'Queen of the Blues', with large, lavender flowers. *C. imperati*, lilac streaked purple, blooms in mid-winter.

POSSIBLE PROBLEMS Mice and birds may damage the corms.

GALANTHUS

spring	hardy	semi-shade	7.5cm/3in	10cm/4in

No garden is complete without snowdrops, one of the first bulbs to flower outdoors. There are several varieties. *Galanthus nivalis* (*above*) is the common snowdrop, with nodding white flowers dotted green, the best for naturalizing in grass or beneath shrubs. Large-flowered varieties are a better choice for the open ground.

GROWING Plant the fresh bulbs as soon as they are available: snowdrops can be difficult to establish and the bulbs must not dry out. Set them in moisture-retentive loam in a position where they will receive good light in very early spring.

PROPAGATION Once established, snowdrops multiply freely. Lift and divide the clusters while in flower or just afterwards and replant immediately. Separate each bulb carefully so that its leaves and roots are undamaged. Plants may be raised from seed – in fact thriving plants may self-seed – and take 5 years to reach maturity.

SPECIES *G. nivalis reginae-olgae*, sub-species, flowers in autumn before the leaves appear; *G. n.* 'Flore-Plena', double, showy flowers; *G. n.* 'Viridapicis', large flowers, green spot on both outer and inner petals; *G. elwesii*, up to 25cm/10in high, spring-flowering, green inner petals.

POSSIBLE PROBLEMS Bulb eelworm; narcissus fly maggots; grey mould on leaves.

▨ PROPAGATION TIP

When bulbs are left to naturalize, do not cut the grass for at least 6 weeks after the flowers have faded so the bulbs can store food for next year's blooms.

▨ PLANTING TIP

Plant bulbs in clumps, rather than strung out in rows: they look much more effective when massed together (this applies to all bulbs). Bulbs are very good if you are short of space, as even one tub crammed with bulbs will brighten up a patio or balcony.

MUSCARI

| spring | hardy | full sun | 20cm/8in | 7.5cm/3in |

The intense blue of the tightly packed little flower clusters of the grape hyacinth rivals gentians in richness. They look best in clumps at the edge of a border and last well as cut flowers.

GROWING Set out bulbs 7.5cm/3in deep from late summer to autumn, in well-drained, reasonably fertile soil. Plants grown in shade will produce excessive foliage at the expense of flowers.

PROPAGATION Clumps need dividing every 3 years or they become overcrowded. Just after flowering or when dormant, lift, divide and replant parent bulbs and offsets immediately.

SPECIES *Muscari armeniacum (above)*, 7.5cm/3in long spikes of violet-blue flowers; the variety 'Early Giant' bears electric blue blooms, while 'Cantab' is pale blue; *M. botryoides*: only 10cm/4in high, deep blue flowers, early spring; the variety 'Album' is pure white; *M. tubergenianum*, the Oxford and Cambridge grape hyacinth, is so called because the upper flowers are much paler than the lower, rich blue ones.

POSSIBLE PROBLEMS Generally trouble-free.

CHIONODOXA

| spring | hardy | full sun | 15cm/6in | 7.5cm/3in |

The chionodoxa or glory-of-the-snow is a member of the lily family. It bears open, five-petalled flowers of pale blue or violet with white centres. Like the crocus, snowdrop and grape hyacinth, chionodoxa looks attractive in small groups and at the edge of a border. Indeed these four species do very well planted together in intermingling clumps.

GROWING Plant bulbs in autumn 7.5cm/3in deep in groups in moisture-retentive soil. No further attention is needed until the plants are overcrowded and need dividing.

PROPAGATION Lift, divide, and replant offsets as the foliage is dying down. Alternatively collect seed in spring when ripe (black) but before the seed box has split, and sow immediately in a frame or nursery bed. Transfer seedlings to the flowering site in the second summer.

SPECIES *C. luciliae (above)*, deep blue flowers with white eye, 2.5cm/1in across; varieties include 'Rosea', pink and 'Wanenburg', bright blue; *C. gigantea*, large, lilac flowers; the variety 'Alba' is pure white.

POSSIBLE PROBLEMS Slugs may eat flowers and leaves.

▓ PLANTING TIP

An ideal spring bulb for early colour. Use in containers, beds, window-boxes, or plant as edging. If naturalizing in grass remember it spreads quickly.

▓ PLANTING TIPS

Bulbs make a good showing in tubs and containers on the patio, as well as in borders. Chionodoxas are good spring-flowering bulbs which can be planted under or around permanent shrubs or flowers in a tub, providing early colour on your patio and garden.

TULIPA

| spring | hardy | full sun | 10cm/4in | 7.5cm/3in |

Tulips were introduced to Europe from Turkey in the 16th century and have been firm favourites ever since. Most of the cultivated forms now seen are hybrids classified into 14 divisions according to their characteristics. Division 15 comprises the exquisite species tulips, many of which are ideal for rock gardens and containers. The colour range is extensive.

GROWING Plant bulbs 15cm/6in deep in late autumn in groups of 6-12 in well-drained soil in a site sheltered from wind. After flowering, remove the dead leaves and stems. Most species can be left in the ground to flower in subsequent years. Keep free of weeds. Bulbs that must be lifted should be stored in boxes in a dry shed.

PROPAGATION Lift the bulbs carefully when the leaves turn yellow. Remove the offsets, grade by size (discarding the very smallest) and store until planting time at 16-18°C/61-64°F. Replant small offsets 5cm/2in deep.

SPECIES *Tulipa urumiensis* (*above*); *T. tarda* (*above*) forms a rosette of leaves at the base of the stem, with several bright yellow blooms, tipped white, from each cluster; *T. greigii*, height 23cm/9in, vivid scarlet, pointed petals, leaves streaked dark red; *T. pulchella*, violet-red flowers, narrow leaves tinged red; must be lifted.

POSSIBLE PROBLEMS Mice may eat bulbs in store. See also other tulip entries.

▓ SPECIAL CARE TIP

Tulips are not difficult, but they should be planted slightly later than other bulbs – in late autumn/early winter. The bulbs can be left in the ground, but most will improve with being lifted every year and stored. Leave in the ground or container until the foliage has turned yellow, then store in a frost-free shed or cellar.

DARWIN TULIPS

| spring | hardy | full sun | 60cm/24in | 15cm/6in |

Darwin tulips, classified division 6, are those most often used in formal bedding schemes. Their large, rounded flowers – 10-15cm/4-6in across – are available in a dazzling range of colours and are held erect on strong stems. They have been crossed with the species *T. fosteriana*, which has grey-green leaves and huge scarlet flowers, to produce Darwin hybrids (Division 5). Tulips in this group are vividly colourful with the largest blooms of all.

GROWING Plant the bulbs late in the autumn to avoid young growth being damaged by frost. Tulips like an alkaline environment; add ground limestone before planting on acid soils. Set the bulbs 15cm/6in deep, more on light soil. Planting distance can be varied for effect as when interplanting with wallflowers as shown. Lift and store when the foliage turns yellow.

PROPAGATION Remove offsets when lifting, grade by size (discarding the smallest) and store at 16-18°C/61-64°F until replanting.

VARIETIES Div. 5: 'Beauty of Appeldoorn' (*above*), yellow within, outside flushed red; 'General Eisenhower', vivid scarlet; 'Jewel of Spring', sharp yellow, spotted red, black base; Div. 6: 'Glacier', ivory; 'Margaux', wine red; 'Reliance', lilac shaded silver; 'Scarlett O'Hara', bright red.

POSSIBLE PROBLEMS Virus diseases such as cucumber mosaic virus. Damaged bulbs may develop mould in store.

▓ CUT FLOWER TIP

Cut thick-stemmed flowers like these under water, and cut at an angle, so that the stems do not sit on the bottom of the vase and fail to take up water.

PARROT TULIPS

| spring | hardy | full sun | 45cm/18in | 15cm/6in |

Parrot tulips differ from the smooth-petalled, cup-shaped symmetry of most types, having petals that are often attractively fringed and twisted. Many varieties are bi-coloured: these colour 'breaks', originally caused by virus infections, were once greatly admired and became fashionable enough to constitute a single group, Division 10. Division 9, Rembrandt tulips, are Darwins with colour breaks. Both are great favourites with flower arrangers.

GROWING Plant bulbs 15cm/6in deep in late autumn, in alkaline soil. Lift and store when the foliage turns yellow.

PROPAGATION Remove offsets when lifting, grade by size (discarding the smallest) and store at 16-18°C/61-64°F until replanting.

VARIETIES Div 10: 'Black Parrot' *(above)*, very dark purple; 'Gadelan', violet splashed green, white base; 'White Parrot', pure white; 'Texas Gold', deep yellow, narrow red edge; 'Orange Parrot', deep orange, mahogany within, richly scented. Div. 9: 'American Flag', deep red and white; 'Zomerschoon', coral pink and cream.

POSSIBLE PROBLEMS *See left*. Very dry soils may well cause 'blindness' – the flowers wither before opening. Grey bulb rot destroys bulbs.

DOUBLE TULIPS

| spring | hardy | full sun | 30-60cm/12-24in | 15cm/6in |

The large, showy blooms of double-flowering tulips resemble peonies. Up to 10cm/4in across, they open wide and flat, looking spectacular on their stiff stems. Division 2, Early Doubles, are so-called because they can be forced to flower indoors for winter decoration. Double Lates, Division 11, earn their name because they stay in bloom for a long time unless damaged by bad weather.

GROWING Plant bulbs 15cm/6in deep in late autumn, in alkaline soil. Lift and store when the foliage turns yellow.

PROPAGATION Remove offsets when lifting, grade by size (discarding the smallest) and store at 16-18°C/61-64°F until replanting.

VARIETIES Early: 'Dante', blood red; 'Goya', deep coral, flushed yellow; 'Schoonord', pure white, very large; 'Peach Blossom' *(above)*, rose pink on white. Late: 'Mount Tacoma', pure white, strong grower; 'Eros', rose pink, scented; 'Gold Medal', saffron yellow; 'Livingstone', red.

POSSIBLE PROBLEMS *See left*. Tulip fire is a serious fungus disease occurring in cold wet weather.

PLANTING TIP

These brilliantly coloured flowers look most effective planted in a block, rather than strung out in a thin row. This is especially true of the bi-coloured variety.

PLANTING TIP

To force tulips, bury the bulbs in their pots. Dig a trench in the garden 40cm/16in deep. Pot the bulbs with their necks just below the compost and place in the trench. Cover with soil and cover with straw in frosty weather. Check growth in mid-winter and remove from trench when necks are 7cm/23/4in.

ERANTHIS

| winter | hardy | semi-shade | 10cm/4in | 7.5cm/3in |

The winter aconite, *Eranthis hyemalis (above)*, cheerfully bears its rounded, buttercup-like yellow flowers while snow is still on the ground. The stems are leafless, but each flower is surrounded by a neck-ruff of narrow leaves.

GROWING Plant the tubers in late summer, setting them 2.5cm/1in deep in small groups. They are happiest in soil enriched with peat or leaf-mould, preferably nestling beneath shrubs where they can naturalize undisturbed. Keep weed-free and well-watered, especially in spring.

PROPAGATION When the plants start to die down, lift the tubers and cut or break them into small sections. Replant immediately.

VARIETIES There are no named varieties of the species. The hybrid *E. × tubergenii* flowers a little later but bears slightly larger flowers. Named varieties such as 'Guinea Gold' have bronzed foliage.

POSSIBLE PROBLEMS Birds may damage the flowerbuds.

LEUCOJUM

| spring/summer | hardy | semi-shade | 30-45cm/12-18in | 20cm/8in |

There are three species of leucojum in general cultivation. These bulbs bear delicate white flowers rather like a snowdrop but rounder in shape. Leucojums are taller and different species flower in spring, summer and the early autumn. They are not difficult to grow and require minimal attention.

GROWING Plant fresh bulbs in late summer/early autumn 7.5cm/3in deep. *Leucojum aestivum*, the summer snowflake, and *L. vernum*, the spring snowflake, require moisture-retentive soil. *L. autumnale*, the autumn snowflake, prefers free-draining soil and should be set only 5cm/2in deep. Leave the clumps undisturbed for several seasons and divide them when overcrowding reduces the production of flowers.

PROPAGATION Offsets will flower next to the parent bulb, but when they are overcrowded should be lifted, divided and replanted. Lift the bulbs when the foliage has died down.

SPECIES *L. aestivum (above)*, rich green strap-like leaves, white flowers tipped green, late spring; *L. autumnale*, grass-like foliage appears after the small, pure white blooms, late summer; *L. vernum*, only 15cm/6in high, single white flowers, tipped green, early spring.

POSSIBLE PROBLEMS Generally trouble-free.

■ PLANTING TIP

All bulbs need moisture while growing, but because they are fleshy they will not tolerate waterlogged conditions. Plant where drainage is good.

■ PLANTING TIP

L. aestivum, the summer-flowering variety, likes a moisture-retaining soil, unlike most bulbs. It is ideal, therefore, for planting in a bog garden , *or for enlivening an otherwise dull, damp and shady corner of the garden.*

CYCLAMEN

| summer | hardy | semi-shade | 10cm/4in | 10-15cm/4-6in |

Hardy cyclamens are cousins of the familiar flowering house-plant *Cyclamen persicum*. They are diminutive but charming plants and once established they flower for years. The beautifully marked foliage makes long-lasting ground cover in shady corners. *C. neapolitanum (above)* is the best species for this purpose, with flowers in various shades of pink appearing from late summer to late autumn. The deep green leaves are variable in shape – the alternative name, *C. hederifolium*, reflects their occasional resemblance to ivy – but are always streaked silver, and red on the underside.

GROWING Plant the tubers in late summer/early autumn in clusters barely covered with soil. Well-drained soil containing plenty of well-rotted organic matter is best. Choose a shady site sheltered from wind. Mulch annually with a 2.5cm/1in layer of leaf mould when the foliage has died down.

PROPAGATION As offsets are not produced, cyclamens must be increased from seed. Collect ripe seed in summer and sow in early autumn in pots of seed compost kept in a ventilated cold frame. Prick the seedlings out into small pots of potting compost. Overwinter in a cold frame and plant out in late spring.

VARIETIES *C. n.* 'Album' is a white form.

POSSIBLE PROBLEMS Generally trouble-free.

HYACINTHUS

| spring | hardy | full sun | 30cm/12in | 23cm/9in |

The hyacinth bears spikes of fragrant flowers of white, blue, yellow, pink or red in early spring. Most of the generally available varieties belong to the group called Dutch hybrids, developed from the species *Hyacinthus orientalis*. They are commercially forced into flowering early for indoor plants, but are ideal for spring flowering outdoors in more formal schemes.

GROWING Plant the bulbs as soon as they are available in early autumn, in rich, well-drained soil. A sunny site is important if you want the bulbs to bloom for more than one year.

PROPAGATION Hyacinths are not prolific, but offsets can be taken from the parent bulb, which should be lifted after the foliage has died down. Replant the bulbils immediately.

VARIETIES Recommended for bedding: 'King of the Blues', deep blue; 'La Victoire', red; 'Pink Pearl' (*above*), deep pink; 'L'Innocence', white; 'City of Haarlem', primrose yellow.

POSSIBLE PROBLEMS Stem and bulb eelworm; narcissus fly maggots.

■ PLANTING TIP

This attractive bulb will last for years and is ideal for naturalizing. Choose a shady corner where it can stay undisturbed and it will provide excellent ground cover with its decorative leaves.

■ PLANTING TIP

To avoid bulbs rotting in heavy soils, improve drainage by planting bulbs in a 30cm/12in hole half filled with grit or fine gravel. Cover bulbs with soil.

Narcissus Hybrids

| spring | hardy | full sun | 25-45cm /10-18in | 15cm/6in |

Everyone can put a name to the cheerful daffodil, but few realize what an enormous number of species and hybrids are available. All bear six-petalled flowers with a trumpet-shaped central corona. Those with a corona as long as, or longer than, the petals are known as daffodils, the others as narcissi. The corona may be deeper in colour than the petals; both are usually a shade of yellow, but white, cream and pale pink varieties have been developed. Narcissi are divided into 11 groups, which include thousands of named varieties.

GROWING Plant bulbs in autumn in a hole three times the depth of the bulb, deeper if in a bed which will be cultivated through the year, where the hoe might damage the bulbs. Divide the clumps when overcrowded. Do not tie up the leaves after flowering.

PROPAGATION Lift the bulbs when the leaves are beginning to turn yellow. Remove and replant the offsets.

VARIETIES 'Suzy' *(above)*, jonquil type, pale yellow and orange; 'Texas', double-flowered, yellow and deep orange; 'Thalia', triandrus type, with several white, nodding flowers per stem.

POSSIBLE PROBLEMS Narcissus fly; stem eelworm; slugs.

Narcissus Species

| spring | hardy | semi-shade | 20cm/8in | 20cm/8in |

Species of wild daffodils are generally smaller than the cultivated hybrids and the flower form is very varied. Most do well in the open, left alone to flower for many years. Some are good for rock gardens. Varieties suitable for naturalizing in grass, for which narcissi are perhaps the ideal subject, are described below.

GROWING Naturalized narcissi do best in rich soil, protected by the shade of larger plants such as trees and shrubs. Soil should not be waterlogged or too dry. Plant in late summer with random spacing; scatter the bulbs on the ground and plant them where they fall, in holes three times the depth of the bulb.

PROPAGATION If necessary, lift and divide the bulbs after flowering and replant immediately.

SPECIES *Narcissus cyclamineus 'February Gold' (above)*, early-flowering species with rich yellow, swept-back flowers; in moist soil it will seed and increase freely; best in fine grass. *N. pseudonarcissus*, the wild daffodil or lent lily, up to 30cm/12in high, creamy petals with lemon trumpets; the better choice for tall grass.

POSSIBLE PROBLEMS Given suitable conditions, naturalized narcissi are relatively trouble-free.

▆ PROPAGATION TIP

If you want to lift bulbs after flowering to make room for other plants, carefully dig them up and heel in elsewhere until the foliage dies down.

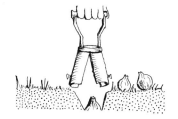

▆ PLANTING TIP

Bulbs for naturalizing are best planted with a bulb planter. This tool removes a core of soil, and you then place the bulb in the hole and replace the soil 'plug'.

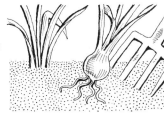

IRIS SPECIES

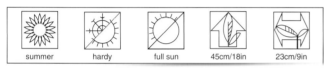

| summer | hardy | full sun | 45cm/18in | 23cm/9in |

The iris family includes a great number of species and hybrids, with very beautiful flowers of blue or yellow in a distinctive arrangement of petals but varying greatly in size and use. Most irises grow from rhizomes, a few from true bulbs. Several are excellent rock garden plants; those described here are ideal for waterside planting or moist conditions.

GROWING Plant rhizomes in spring or late summer at the water's edge or in water up to 45cm/18in deep, depending on species. The clumps should be lifted every 3 years for division

PROPAGATION Just after flowering, lift the rhizomes and divide by cutting off pieces from the outside of the clump, discarding the centre. Each piece should have one or two good fans of leaves. Replant immediately.

SPECIES I. laevigata (above), deep blue flowers up to 15cm/6in across, water depth 15cm/6in; named varieties include 'Alba', pure white and 'Monstrosa', white blotched purple. I. pseudocorus, reaches up to 1.2m/4ft in 45cm/18in of water, half that height in a damp border; vivid yellow blooms; named varieties need only 15cm/6in water. I. versicolor, violet flowers, ideal lakeside plant in 7.5cm/3in water; 'Kermesina' is a wine-red variety.

POSSIBLE PROBLEMS Cucumber mosaic virus; leaf spot; iris sawfly.

IRIS BULBS

| summer | hardy | full sun | 60cm/24in | 15cm/6in |

Bulbous irises are a small group which include the dwarf reticulated types ideal for rockeries and pot culture. For general garden cultivation hybrids of the xiphium group are best. These fall into three categories: Dutch irises are first to flower in early summer; the Spanish irises bloom about 2 weeks later, and finally the English irises 2 weeks later still. All come in a range of delectable colours, but the English group, while it bears flowers 12.5cm/5in across, contains no yellows.

GROWING Plant the bulbs in autumn 10 15cm/4 6in deep, in light, fertile soil in the case of Dutch and Spanish hybrids. The English hybrids like rich, damp soil.

PROPAGATION Lift the bulbs after flowering. Detach the offsets and replant immediately, placing the smallest specimens in a nursery bed for a year.

VARIETIES Dutch: 'Golden Harvest', vivid yellow; 'National Velvet', deep purple, blotched orange. Spanish: 'Frederika', white blotched yellow; 'Blue River', aquamarine blotched orange. English: 'Prince Albert', silvery blue; 'Mirabeau', purple blotched white.

POSSIBLE PROBLEMS Narcissus fly larvae; grey bulb rot.

▨ PLANTING TIP

There are almost too many irises to choose from, as there is a different type for every spot in the garden, from the herbaceous border to the edge of a pond. It is essential to know what type you want before buying and to buy with a definite spot in the garden in mind.

▨ PLANTING TIP

Some varieties of the dwarf bulb iris will tolerate a dry soil, and so can be used for underplanting shrubs and trees, such as twisted hazel. The dwarf bulb iris is also ideal for brightening up tubs and containers in spring, as well as for rock gardens.

IPHEION

| spring | hardy | sun/semi-shade | 15cm/6in | 7.5cm/3in |

A member of the lily family, *Ipheion uniflorum* is native to South America. It is also known as *Brodiaea* or *Triteleia uniflora*. When closely grouped, the star-shaped flowers of white or shades of blue make an attractive addition to the front of the border. While the flowers have a pleasant scent, the leaves smell faintly of garlic.

GROWING Plant bulbs 2.5-5cm/1-2in deep in late autumn in well-drained soil. Choose a sheltered site. Ipheions prefer sun but tolerate partial shade. Remove dead flower stems and foliage in late summer. To prevent overcrowding lift and divide the clumps every 2-3 years.

PROPAGATION Ipheions produce offsets freely. Lift the bulbs as the leaves are fading, separate the offsets and replant immediately.

VARIETIES 'Violacea' (*above*), violet-blue; 'Caeruleum', pale blue.

POSSIBLE PROBLEMS Generally trouble-free.

FREESIA

| summer | half-hardy | full sun | 45-60cm/18-24in | 10cm/4in |

Freesias are members of the iris family native to South Africa. The hybrid *Freesia × kewensis* is commercially cultivated in greenhouse conditions for its colourful, scented blooms on slender stems. Specially treated corms are available which will flower outdoors in mid-summer, but only for one season. In favoured areas ordinary, untreated corms can be used and will flower for several years.

GROWING Plant prepared corms in spring, 7.5cm/3in deep in well-drained, moderately fertile soil on a sheltered site. Even then, twiggy sticks will probably be necessary for support. Lift the corms when the foliage dies down. In warm areas, plant ordinary corms in late summer and leave in the ground after flowering.

PROPAGATION Offsets removed when lifting the corms can be brought to flower in cool greenhouse conditions in subsequent years.

VARIETIES 'Margret' (*above*), purplish-pink veined purple; 'Klondyke', yellow shading to gold; 'Snow Queen', cream with yellow throat; 'Stockholm', red with yellow throat.

POSSIBLE PROBLEMS Aphids and caterpillars damage leaves and young shoots.

◼ PLANTING TIP

This attractive little plant looks very good in a rock garden, and it will appreciate an open, sunny position. Remember to divide clumps and detach offsets in autumn, to prevent overcrowding.

◼ SPECIAL CARE TIP

A joy to grow because of their scent, outdoor freesias do need a warm, dry spot to flower well in late summer and autumn. They also need to be kept watered, but at the same time avoid planting in heavy, waterlogged soil. Like all bulbs, they will do best on well-drained fertile soil.

COLCHICUM

autumn	hardy	full sun	15cm/6in	23cm/9in

The autumn crocus is not in fact related to the crocus, though they look similar when in flower. Colchicums are members of the lily family (crocuses belong to the iris family), with oval (not flat) corms and long, rather untidy leaves. This feature should be borne in mind when choosing a planting site, as the leaves persist long after the flowers have died down. As they can be left undisturbed for years, it is a good idea to group them in rough grass.

GROWING Plant the corms in late summer in any type of well-drained soil. Set them 10cm/4in deep in small groups. Lift and divide when overcrowded.

PROPAGATION Lift the corms in summer, detach the offsets and replant immediately.

SPECIES *C. speciosum (above)*, flowers in shades of mauve. Beautiful hybrids developed from the species include 'The Giant', large mauve flowers, white centre; 'Album', pure white; 'Atrorubens', crimson-purple.

POSSIBLE PROBLEMS Slugs may eat the corms and leaves.

SCILLA

spring	hardy	sun/semi-shade	15cm/6in	7.5cm /3in

These hardy bulbs belong to the useful group of spring-flowering plants which are simplicity to grow yet produce brilliantly coloured blooms to brighten the border or create a splash of colour in grass. Most scillas, or squills to give them their common name, bear their star-shaped flowers in varying shades of blue. The shiny leaves are mid-green and precede the flower stems.

GROWING Plant the bulbs 5-7.5cm/2-3in deep in moist well-drained soil in late summer. A sunny or partially shaded position will do. Leave the bulbs undisturbed thereafter.

PROPAGATION Scillas produce their offsets slowly. Their presence is indicated by extra clusters of leaves. Lift the bulbs carefully after the foliage has died down, detach the offsets and replant immediately. They may not flower the first year.

SPECIES *S. sibirica*, 3-4 stems per bulb, brilliant blue flowers; *S. tubergeniana (above)*, very early-flowering, pale blue flowers, good in mixed spring planting; *S. peruviana*, flowers early summer, 23cm/9in high, profuse, intensely blue flowers.

POSSIBLE PROBLEMS Yellow spots on the leaves may be caused by rust.

■ ORGANIC TIP

Bulbs left to naturalize in grass will enjoy a feed of liquid manure after flowering. If in a bed, mulch soil with well-rotted manure after foliage has died down.

■ PLANTING TIP

Spring bulbs can be left to naturalize under trees and shrubs, but ideally the bulbs should flower before the shade from the leaves becomes too dense.

DAHLIA

| summer/autumn | half-hardy | sun/semi-shade | 45cm/18in | 45-60cm/18-24in |

Long-lasting and excellent for cutting, dahlias are among the most popular summer flowers. The types grown from tubers are called border dahlias, which are divided into groups, namely: Single-flowered; Anemone-flowered; Collerette (with a collar of smaller florets); Peony-flowered; Decorative (large ray florets, reminiscent of chrysanthemums); Ball; Pompon; Cactus and Semi-cactus (pointed petals). Decorative, Ball and Cactus dahlias are further subdivided by size. The colour range is wide, excluding blue, but all shades have a characteristic clarity and brightness. Dahlias are in glorious bloom from high summer until the first frosts. The minimum height is given above – some varieties reach 1.5m/5ft.

GROWING Dahlias are best grown in a special bed on well-drained soil previously enriched with well-rotted organic matter. Just before planting, rake in bonemeal at 100g/m² (4oz/sq.yd). Place a stake in each planting hole to support the stem to within 30cm/12in of its ultimate height. Plant unsprouted tubers in spring, 12.5cm/5in deep. Plant sprouted tubers in late spring or wait until summer in cold wet seasons. As the plants grow, tie the stems loosely to the stakes. For additional growing advice, see next entry.

DAHLIA

| summer | half-hardy | sun/semi-shade | 45cm/18in | 45-60cm/18-24in |

When dahlias are grown for exhibition purposes, a process of disbudding is carried out to produce fewer, larger flowers. This is not necessary in normal circumstances, but it is advisable to pinch out the leading shoots once, a month after planting. Lift and store the tubers annually. Raise them carefully, using a spade, a week after frost has turned the leaves black. Drain off water from the stems. Store healthy tubers only. Place them in boxes, just covered with peat, in a frostproof place. Inspect from time to time to make sure none is affected by mould.

PROPAGATION Set overwintered tubers in boxes of peat and sand in spring, with the crowns visible. Keep moist and frost-free. When the 'eyes' begin to swell, cut the tubers into pieces, each with an eye, and pot up or plant 10cm/4in deep in a cold frame. Plant out when danger of frost is passed.

VARIETIES Single: 'Sion', bronze; Anemone: 'Lucy', purple, yellow centre; Collerette: 'Can-Can', pink, yellow inner ring; Decorative: 'Little Tiger', red and cream, dwarf; Ball: 'Gloire de Lyon', white; Pompon: 'Nero', maroon; Cactus: 'Bach', yellow.

POSSIBLE PROBLEMS Aphids, caterpillars, earwigs; grey mould, petal blight.

▦ PLANTING TIP

Dahlias are best planted in a bed on their own, to make an effective display. They are also useful for providing late colour in a border when most other flowers are fading or dying back. Taller varieties are available for the back of the border, while smaller ones, like 'Lilliput', will bloom in the front till the first frosts.

▦ ORGANIC TIP

Dust tubers with sulphur before planting, to discourage any fungal attack. Set slug traps or use organic slug powder to avoid damage to new shoots.

LILIUM SPECIES

summer	hardy	sun or partial shade	1.2-1.8m/4-6ft	30cm/12in

In spite of its majestic, exotic appearance, the lily is generally not difficult to grow. The numerous species and hybrids are divided into 9 groups according to origin, with true species in Division 9. All lily bulbs, made up of tightly packed scales, produce roots from the base, but some also have roots from the stems; this type should be planted deeper than basal-rooting bulbs. Flowers may be trumpet-shaped, bowl-shaped or, in the form called Turk's-cap, with recurved petals. The colour range is very wide, excluding blue.

GROWING Plant fresh bulbs from autumn to spring (basal rooting bulbs always in autumn), about 15cm/6in deep depending on size. A south-facing site sheltered from wind is best; ordinary well-drained soil will do. While some species dislike lime, others prefer it. Enrich soil with well-rotted organic matter before planting.

PROPAGATION Some lilies produce numerous offsets which may be treated in the usual way. Scale propagation (*see right*) is suitable for all types.

SPECIES *Lilium regale* (*above*), China, fragrant, white, trumpet flowers 15cm/6in long, stem-rooting bulbs which increase quickly; *L. pardalinum* (panther lily), California, 5cm/2in orange-red Turk's-cap flowers, basal rooting bulb, needs lime-free soil.

POSSIBLE PROBLEMS Leatherjackets; lily beetle larvae.

▦ PLANTING TIP

The blooms of these summer-flowering bulbs like sunshine, but the roots prefer shade. Ideally, plant the bulbs at the foot of a low-growing shrub.

LILIUM HYBRIDS

summer	hardy	sun/semi-shade	60cm-2.1m/2-7ft	15-30cm/6-12in

The many hybrid lilies raised from species are broadly grouped as Asiatic, European or American, and include countless stunning varieties.

GROWING Plant from autumn to spring about 15cm/6in deep depending on size. Lilies like well-drained soil enriched with well-rotted organic matter and a sheltered, sunny site.

PROPAGATION In spring or autumn, scrape away earth from the dormant bulbs and gently remove healthy scales. Replace the soil. Place scales at an angle in boxes of peat and sand to half their depth. Set in a cold frame at 10°C/50°F. New bulbs form at the base of the scales. When shoots form on these tiny bulbils, pot them up in compost and transfer to an open frame or sheltered bed. Transplant to permanent positions 2-3 years later.

HYBRIDS 'Orange Triumph' (*above*), from *L. × hollandicum* (formerly *L. × umbellatum*), upright cup-shaped flowers. The Mid-Century group, to 1.5m/5ft, includes 'Cinnabar', maroon; 'Joan Evans', bright yellow; 'Valencia', soft orange. The fine American Bellingham hybrids reach up to 2.1m/7ft and include 'Royal Favorite', Chinese yellow speckled deep red. 'Parkmanni' is an outstanding American lily with open, very fragrant flowers up to 30cm/12in in diameter, crimson inside, rose outside, tinged green and white.

POSSIBLE PROBLEMS Basal rot; lily disease.

▦ PLANTING TIP

There is an enormous variety of these hybrids to choose from, in all kinds of colours and sizes. The bulbs must never be allowed to dry out, so plant immediately after purchase. Mid-autumn is best for planting lilium, when the soil is still free of frost.

BEGONIA

summer	half-hardy	full sun	20-60cm/8-24in	30cm/12in

The smooth, rounded leaves of tuberous begonia hybrids (*Begonia × tuberhybrida*) make a perfect foil for their large, rose-like flowers. The colour range includes white, yellow, pink, orange and red. Pendula hybrids, with slightly drooping stems, are seen to best advantage in hanging baskets or window-boxes.

GROWING Start tubers into growth in spring in boxes of moist peat at 18°C/64°F. Pot on into 12.5cm/5in pots of compost when leafy shoots appear, then into 20cm/8in pots. Plant outdoors in early summer in well-drained soil previously enriched with peat or leaf mould. Lift before the first frosts and overwinter at 7°C/45°F, just covered with dry peat.

PROPAGATION In spring, when potting up, divide the tubers into pieces bearing at least one healthy shoot each. Treat as above.

VARIETIES 'Single White' (*above*); 'Buttermilk', cream; 'Festiva', rich yellow; 'Margaret Collins', true pink; 'Ninette', pale apricot, very large; 'T. B. Toop', orange; 'Olympia', deep scarlet, Pendula hybrid; 'Dawn', buff-yellow; 'Yellow Sweetie', lemon, lightly scented.

POSSIBLE PROBLEMS Weevils, eelworms, tarsonemid mites; grey mould.

GLADIOLUS

summer	half-hardy	full sun	60-90cm/2-3ft	15cm/6in

Gladioli bear their lily-like flowers on one side of an erect spike. Large-flowered hybrids are the best choice for the garden border; for cutting, choose Primulinus hybrids, 45-90cm/18in-3ft high, or Miniatures, the same height but with numerous smaller florets. The colour range is breathtaking, including both bright and subtle shades, but no blues.

GROWING Dig a layer of well-rotted manure into the site in early spring. Rake bonemeal into the surface at 75g/m² (3oz/sq. yd). Plant corms 10cm/4in deep, more in light soil, in spring. If the corms are not deep enough the mature plants may keel over. Space gladioli for cutting in rows 30cm/12in apart. Keep weed-free. Do not water for 8-10 weeks, then water generously. When the foliage yellows lift the corms and cut off the main stem to 1cm/½in. Dry off in warmth and store in a cool frost-free place.

PROPAGATION Detach cormlets from the base of the parent and treat in the same way, raising them in nursery beds and storing over winter until they reach flowering size in the second year.

VARIETIES Large-flowered: 'Peter Pears' (*above*), salmon pink; Primulinus: 'Apex', warm red; Miniature: 'Greenbird', sulphur green.

POSSIBLE PROBLEMS Thrips, soil pests, gladiolus dry rot.

PLANTING TIP

The Pendula hybrid, with its drooping stems, is ideal for window-boxes or hanging baskets provided the soil is rich enough and kept watered during flowering.

SPECIAL CARE TIP

The one problem with gladiolus is that the flowers have such a short life, making them unsuitable for a mixed border. They are best grown in a special bed where they can be staked and cared for individually. Stagger the planting of the corms through spring to ensure a steady supply of blooms in the summer.

FRITILLARIA

| spring | hardy | sun/semi-shade | 75cm/30in | 20cm/8in |

The small group of fritillaries in general cultivation range from the majestic *F. imperialis* (crown imperial), which may reach 90cm/3ft, to the 30cm/12in *F. meleagris* (snake's-head fritillary) with its distinctive checkerboard petals. The proud blooms of *F. imperialis*, coronets held high on straight stems clothed with glossy leaves, are best appreciated in a border. *F. meleagris*, by contrast, with its nodding, bell-like flowers, is suited to a semi-wild or at least informal setting.

GROWING Both species like fertile, well-drained soil. *F. imperialis* needs sun. *F. meleagris* does well in moist conditions, in short grass or at the border's edge. Set the bulbs on their sides to prevent water lodging in the depression on top. Plant them in autumn, 20cm/8in deep for *F. imperialis*, 10cm/4in for *F. meleagris*. Do not disturb for at least 4 years, apart from cutting down the stems after flowering.

PROPAGATION Take offsets from mature bulbs after the leaves have withered. Replant bulbils and parent bulbs immediately.

VARIETIES *F. imperialis*: 'Aurora', deep orange; 'Lutea Maxima' (*above*), golden yellow. *F. meleagris*: 'Alba', white, veined green; 'Artemis', purple-grey with purple checkers; 'Saturnus', violet-red.

POSSIBLE PROBLEMS Generally trouble-free.

ZANTEDESCHIA

| summer | half-hardy | full sun | 45cm/18in | 30cm/12in |

Native to South Africa, most species of zantedeschia are grown as greenhouse plants in temperate zones. The exception is *Zantedeschia aethiopica*, the calla lily or arum lily, which – if in pots – can be set outside in the summer, or – in a border or at the water's edge – left outside all year. These are exceptionally beautiful plants, with thick glossy leaves and large white flower spathes.

GROWING Pots: set rhizomes 7.5cm/3in deep in 25cm/10in pots of compost in early spring. Water in, and keep moist at 5°C/41°F minimum until growth appears. Increase watering gradually and feed with liquid fertilizer weekly in summer. Move pots outside in mid summer. Bring inside in autumn and repot in fresh soil. Outdoors: as a water plant *Z. aethiopica* needs 15-30cm/6-12in water. In the open ground, very rich soil is needed. In water or in the border, protect the plants from frost with a layer of bracken or straw.

PROPAGATION Divide the rhizomes when repotting or lift and divide outdoor plants in autumn. Replant immediately.

VARIETIES 'Crowborough', hardier than the species, recommended for outdoor cultivation.

POSSIBLE PROBLEMS Corm rot.

░ PLANTING TIP

F. imperialis, *with its·tall stems and imposing flower-heads, is a real eye-catcher. For maximum effect, plant six or seven together, at the back of the border.*

░ PLANTING TIP

If you have only a patio or balcony to grow flowers in, a mixed selection of zantedeschia plants would make a stunning display and cheer up even the dullest spot. It is best raised indoors or in a greenhouse or conservatory and put outside in pots in summer.

ALPINES

The strict definition of an alpine plant is one that is native to the alpine zone – the area between the end of the tree line and the beginning of the snow line. More loosely interpreted, the term is used to describe any small plant suitable for the rock garden.

What these plants have in common, as well as their jewel-like beauty and diminutive size, is the need for good drainage. Because they look best planted together, and have similar needs, alpine plants are not dotted around the garden – where their unique charms might well be overshadowed by larger varieties – but are given a special place of their own. This may take one of several forms, including that of the rock garden proper.

In order to succeed, a rock garden must look as natural as possible. This means positioning the rocks (and they must be rocks, not rubble) so that only two-thirds of each one can be seen protruding from the soil; often rocks are tilted at an angle, but if so each one should be set to the same degree. They must be distributed on a slope. If your garden does not have a sloping corner in the sun, you can build one, making sure that for every 30cm/12in of height the rock garden extends 1.2m/4ft wide.

Building a rock garden is hard work and achieving a successful design undoubtedly takes talent. A rather easier alternative is a raised bed, which can be of any size as long as it is 60cm/24in above the ground. Raised beds look best if irregular in shape, with the sides treated as a dry wall. They are, incidentally, well suited to elderly or disabled gardeners.

Whether you take up the challenge of a rockery or opt for a raised bed, you must provide at least 30cm/12in of drainage material. Dig out the soil an extra 30cm/12in deep and fill it up with clinker, gravel or rough stones. Construct the rockery or raised bed a layer at a time, filling each one with a compost made up of 3 parts (by volume) loam (or any good garden soil), 2 parts peat, compost or leaf-mould and 3 parts sharp sand or fine grit. Add 2.25kg/5lb bonemeal to every 0.75m³/1cu.yd of this mixture. When construction is complete, water well and leave the soil to settle. It will almost certainly need topping up as the level drops. Finally, strew an even, shallow layer of granite chippings over the soil (limestone chippings for lime-loving plants) and leave for 2-3 weeks before planting up so that any annual weeds that appear can be killed off.

You may be lucky enough to inherit a handsome rockery. If not, it takes time, energy and some cost to build one (rocks are not cheap). Fortunately, the lack of a rockery does not mean that you have to give up the pleasure of growing this exquisite group of plants. As long as you observe their paramount need for good drainage, you can also grow them in shallow troughs and pans or even in the cracks between paving stones on patios, paths and steps. Stone troughs look wonderful planted up with a selection of alpine plants. This particular version of container growing makes it possible to

include a wide number of different plants in a confined space, thanks to their small size. You can create a living patchwork of colour, choosing from the list of plants below, or confine yourself to a range of blues and pinks, perhaps – gentians and campanulas, dianthus and primula, beautifully set off by the weathered grey of old stone. Sedums and saxifrages are two of the easiest alpines to grow and make excellent companions in a trough garden.

Most alpines are sold as pot-grown plants which can, in theory, be planted at any time, but autumn and spring are best. Autumn planting allows the plants to establish themselves before winter comes. Spring planting means that the plants will start to grow away at once, but you will not see them at their best until the following year.

Alpines need watering until they are established, but not after that unless there is a long period of drought. In such conditions, water very thoroughly in the evening so that the water can soak through the soil all night.

Many alpine plants, and in particular alyssum, helianthe-

Here, a colourful selection of thymes are happily established over a set of stone steps. Cracks in walls and between paving stones make excellent homes for alpines.

mum, dianthus and veronicas, benefit from being cut back quite severely when flowering is over to encourage fresh growth and keep the plants compact.

Many experienced gardeners have highly prized collections of alpines, but this should not make the novice feel wary of growing them. Indeed, a trough of alpines is a good way to give children a suitable-sized garden of their own. In smaller modern gardens, too, or wherever there is a sunny corner, however tiny, alpines are the perfect choice.

ALPINES FOR CONTAINERS

Alyssum	*Gentiana*	*Saxifraga*
Arabis	*Helianthemum*	*Sedum*
Aubretia	*Juniperus*	*Sisyrinchium*
Campanula	*Primula*	*Veronica*
Dianthus	*Ramonda*	

SEDUM

summer	hardy	full sun	10cm/4in	30cm/12in

Sedum spurium (above) belongs to the large family of succulent plants which includes biting stonecrop, *S. acre*, and that stalwart of the border *S. spectabile*, so attractive to bees. This diminutive perennial species bears deep pink star-shaped flowers on red stems. The rounded leaves cluster low and spread wide, giving ground cover that is both effective and attractive. Unlike *S. acre*, it is not invasive.

GROWING Plant in well-drained soil between autumn and spring. Full sun is essential. Like most sedums, *S. spurium* is drought-resistant. Do not remove the dead stems after flowering. Wait until spring when they can be picked off easily.

PROPAGATION Division is an easy and reliable method of increasing your stock. Divide and replant between autumn and spring.

VARIETIES 'Album', white; 'Schorbusser Blut', deep red, early-flowering.

POSSIBLE PROBLEMS Aphids on stems and leaves; slugs may eat foliage.

THYMUS

summer	hardy	full sun	15-20cm/6-8in	30cm/12in

There are several species of thyme suitable for the rock garden. The leaves of all of them are highly aromatic and two, *Thymus vulgaris* (common thyme, *above*) and *T. × citriodorus*, are used as culinary herbs (thyme is an essential ingredient in bouquets garnis). A perennial and very easy to grow, thyme spreads quickly and makes effective ground cover. The tiny flowers may be pink, red, lilac or white.

GROWING Plant from autumn to spring in well-drained garden soil. Full sun is important. After flowering snip off the faded flowerheads to encourage sturdy growth.

PROPAGATION Divide the plants in spring or late summer and replant at once directly in the flowering site.

SPECIES *T. vulgaris*, narrow, dark green, highly aromatic leaves, lilac flowers; *T. serpyllum* (correctly known as *T. drucei*), grey-green, very spreading leaves, purple flowers; 'Album' is a white form; 'Pink Chintz' bears salmon-pink flowers; *T. × citriodorus*, lemon-scented leaves, short-lived lilac flowers; the leaves of 'Aureus' are bright golden, those of 'Silver Posy' silver.

POSSIBLE PROBLEMS Generally trouble-free.

▦ ORGANIC TIP

An ideal plant for the organic garden, as its bright flowers, full of nectar, will attract hoverflies (which will keep aphids at bay) and other insects.

▦ ORGANIC TIP

Dried thyme is highly aromatic, and as such is an essential ingredient in bouquets garnis; the flowers provide a good source of nectar for insects.

DIANTHUS

| summer | hardy | full sun | 15-23cm/6-9in | 10cm/4in |

The genus *Dianthus* includes garden pinks, border carnations and florists' perpetual-flowering carnations. Many of the so-called species pinks, exquisite perennials for the rock garden, are strongly scented. The narrow leaves are grey-green and the blooms white, red or shades of pink, sometimes with a central eye.

GROWING Set out young plants in spring or autumn, not too deep, in well-drained non-acid soil. Rake bonemeal into the surface just before planting. Water spring plantings in dry weather; keep autumn-planted stock free of fallen leaves. Pinch out the leading shoots in spring to encourage side-shoots. Remove old stems after flowering.

PROPAGATION Take 7.5cm/3in cuttings in summer and insert in a peat/loam/sand mixture in a cold frame until rooted. Pot up individually or transfer to the flowering site.

SPECIES *D. deltoides*, numerous tiny pink or white flowers until autumn, self-seeds freely, tolerates semi-shade; named varieties include 'Brilliancy' (*above*), bright pink, 'Albus', white; *D. caesius* (correct name *D. gratianopolitanus*, cheddar pink), long-lived, spreading, fringed fragrant pink flowers, early summer; 'Flore-pleno' is a double form.

POSSIBLE PROBLEMS Leaf rot in winter.

ZAUSCHNERIA

| summer/autumn | half-hardy | full sun | 30cm/12in | 45-60cm/18-24in |

Californian fuchsias, to give zauschnerias their common name, are sub-shrubby perennials from western North America and Mexico, suitable for hot, sunny positions such as the foot of a sunny wall. In the right conditions they are long-lived plants and produce their vivid red tubular flowers late in summer, persisting into the autumn.

GROWING Plant in late spring or high summer in light, well-drained soil. In cold areas, protect the plants with leaves or bracken over winter. Cut back in spring to just above ground level.

PROPAGATION Clumps may be divided in spring with difficulty. The better method is to take 7.5cm/3in cuttings of basal shoots in late spring. Insert in a peat/sand mixture in a propagator at 16-18°C/61-64°F until rooted. Pot up individually in compost and transfer to a cold frame. Plant out in late summer or the following spring.

SPECIES *Z. californica*, grey-green hairy leaves, sprays of red flowers 2.5cm/1in long; *Z. cana (above)*, distinguished by very narrow leaves.

POSSIBLE PROBLEMS Aphids on young shoots.

■ SPECIAL CARE TIP

Alpine pinks are easy to grow, but there are a few points to remember for success. The plants need full sun, and do not thrive under a damp mulch.

They only need watering after planting in dry weather, or in exceptionally hot summers. Most plants lose their vigour after a few years.

■ SPECIAL CARE TIP

These heat-loving plants are obviously ideal for sunny gardens where the climate is mild all year round. In colder areas it might be

better to grow this plant as a conservatory or greenhouse specimen.

AUBRIETA

| spring | hardy | full sun | 10cm/4in | 45-60cm/18-24in |

It is easy to be dismissive of the ubiquitous *Aubrieta deltoidea* but it is in fact a very valuable plant, providing sweeps of dramatic colour on dry walls or in the rock garden in late spring, and lasting for weeks. The flowers are tiny but abundant, ranging in colour from lilac to deep purple. The plants form fast-spreading mats.

GROWING Plant between autumn and spring in well-drained soil containing some lime. Plants grown on the rock garden should be sheared right back after flowering to keep them neat; if trailing over a wall, just snip off the old stems.

PROPAGATION Divide rooted stems of established plants in autumn and replant immediately.

VARIETIES 'Gurgedyke', old favourite, deep purple; 'Dr Mules', reliable type, violet; 'Bressingham Pink', double, rosy-pink; 'Argenteo-Variegata', lavender flowers, leaves splashed silver.

POSSIBLE PROBLEMS White blister; downy mildew.

VERONICA

| summer | hardy | full sun | 15cm/6in | 30-60cm/12-24in |

The speedwell family includes six alpine species but two of these, *Veronica pectinata* and *V. filiformis*, are invasive. All bear pink or blue flowers in late spring or summer and are excellent on dry walls or as ground cover plants for rock gardens.

GROWING Plant in a sunny position in well-drained soil from autumn to spring.

PROPAGATION Divide all species, except those that are invasive, in spring, and replant immediately.

SPECIES *V. gentianoides (above)*, slender spikes of palest blue in spring; *V. prostrata* , dense spikes of pale blue flowers freely carried in early summer; named varieties include 'Pygmaea', only 5cm/2in high, 'Rosea', deep pink and 'Spode Blue', china blue; *V. cinerea*, mat-forming, with grey-green leaves and clear pink flowers, mid-summer; *V. teucrium*, variable species – choose named varieties such as 'Shirley Blue', deep blue, or 'Trehane', light blue with leaves variegated yellow.

POSSIBLE PROBLEMS Powdery mildew.

▮ PLANTING TIP

Plant alpines in a rock garden in special 'pockets' for each plant among the rocks. Fill the holes with a mixture of soil, peat and grit before planting.

▮ SPECIAL CARE TIP

To avoid mildew it is essential to provide a well-drained site, such as a rock or scree garden. If grown in containers, always place stones in the bottom.

CAMPANULA

summer	hardy	sun/semi-shade	23cm/9in	30cm/12in

Although the common name for campanulas is bell flower, not all the species bear flowers in this form. A number have star-shaped blooms, including two of the best species for rock gardens. *Campanula carpatica (above)* forms neat, bushy tufts of green, heart-shaped leaves and bears abundant blue, pink or white flowers 4cm/1½in across on erect, wiry stems. *C. garganica* is a rewarding choice – over the whole of the summer it bears so many blue flowers that the leaves are hardly visible. Both spread up to 30cm/12in.

GROWING Plant in well-drained soil in sun or partial shade between autumn and spring. Remove flowerheads when faded.

PROPAGATION Take 2.5cm/1in basal cuttings of non-flowering shoots in spring. Place in a peat/sand mixture in a cold frame until rooted. Pot up individually and grow on until planting out in the autumn.

VARIETIES The species are reliable, but good named varieties include: *G. garganica*: 'W. H. Paine', deep blue with a white eye; 'Hirsuta', grey, hairy leaves – protect from damp with an open cloche over winter. *C. carpatica*: 'Ditton Blue', only 15cm/6in high, indigo; 'White Star', 30cm/12in high, pure white; 'Turbinata', compact shape, blue flowers, hairy leaves need winter protection.

POSSIBLE PROBLEMS Rust.

RAMONDA

spring	hardy	semi-shade	10cm/4in	23cm/9in

Ramondas are native to southern and central Europe. Their predilection for shade and enriched soil distinguishes them from many alpine plants and enables gardeners to fill an awkward spot with an unusual and attractive subject. The dark leaves form a rosette on the ground rather like that of the primula, but are very deep green, crinkly and fringed with hairs. The straight stems bear pale mauve, saucer-shaped flowers with prominent yellow stamens.

GROWING Set out young plants in spring in a cool, shady crevice on soil previously enriched with peat or leaf-mould. Put them at a slight angle to prevent water collecting in the rosette of leaves. Do not let plants dry out in hot summer weather.

PROPAGATION Take leaf cuttings in summer, making sure each leaf has a dormant bud at the base. Insert at an angle 2cm/¾in deep in a peat/sand mixture in a cold frame until rooted (about 6 weeks). Pot up individually and grow on in the frame for two winters before planting out.

SPECIES *R. myconii (above)*, most popular species; named varieties are 'Alba', white and 'Rosea', rich pink; *R. serbica*, smaller rosette of leaves, stamens tipped with purple anthers.

POSSIBLE PROBLEMS Slugs may eat the leaves.

▨ PLANTING TIP

The massed display of flowers is most attractive, and makes this plant one of the prettiest choices when dense ground cover is required. *C. carpatica* is ideal for the rock garden, producing bushy leaves and abundant, bright blue bell-shaped flowers over a long period.

▨ SPECIAL CARE TIP

This species is the exception to the rule that rock gardens should be open and in full sun, since this prefers a shady spot. Like other plants which form rosettes, it should be planted at an angle to prevent water collecting in the centre of the rosettes, and should be protected with a mini-cloche in very wet winters.

LITHODORA

summer	hardy	full sun	10cm/4in	60cm/24in

Sometimes listed as *Lithospermum*, the genus *Lithodora* belongs to the same family as forget-me-nots, and, like them, bears bright blue star-shaped flowers. The flowers of *L. diffusa (above)* bloom all summer, emerging from a mat of dark green foliage that makes invaluable ground cover for the rock garden.

GROWING Plant in spring in light soil to which peat or leaf-mould has been added. This species will not tolerate lime.

PROPAGATION In the summer take soft green cuttings 4-6.5cm/1½-2½in long with a heel, and insert in a peat/sand mixture in a shaded frame until rooted. Water regularly. Pot up individually, overwinter in the frame and plant out the following spring.

VARIETIES 'Grace Ward', clear blue; 'Heavenly Blue' (rarely available), profuse, deep blue flowers.

POSSIBLE PROBLEMS Generally trouble-free.

OMPHALODES

spring	hardy	semi-shade	15cm/6in	25cm/10in

Omphalodes verna (above), like lithodora, belongs to the for-get-me-not family. Fortunately it has a common name – blue-eyed mary – which is less of a tongue-twister than the Latin one. Suitable for the rock garden or the front of a border, this early-flowering perennial species forms tufts of long-stalked mid-green leaves with open sprays of bright blue flowers. The plant spreads by means of runners. Its slightly larger relative, *O. cappadocica*, is a clump-forming species that carries dense sprays of sky-blue flowers in early summer.

GROWING Plant in spring in peaty soil. Water generously in hot weather and dead-head regularly to prolong flowering.

PROPAGATION Divide and replant in spring or in summer when flowering is over.

VARIETIES The species are reliable. There is a white-flowered variety of *O. verna* named 'Alba'.

POSSIBLE PROBLEMS Generally trouble-free.

▓ PLANTING TIP

This plant definitely needs an acid soil. If your soil is alkaline, provide a special pocket in the rock garden or wall and fill with a peat mixture before planting.

▓ PLANTING TIP

Although this is described as an alpine, O. verna and O. cappadocica both do well in moist, shady woodland conditions, rather than in the dry, full sun conditions of a rock garden. O. luciliae is best kept in a conservatory or greenhouse as it is tender, and very prone to slug attacks.

PHACELIA

| summer | hardy | full sun | 23cm/9in | 15cm/6in |

Phacelia campanularia, or California bluebell, is an annual plant whose bright blue, bell-shaped flowers bloom all summer and are attractive to bees. The dark green, rounded leaves are fragrant when crushed. Annuals are useful in the rock garden for introducing a change of colour for one season, or for filling a gap if a perennial becomes exhausted. This species is also good at the front of a border. There are no named varieties.

GROWING Well-drained, well-cultivated sandy soil is best, in a sunny situation.

PROPAGATION Sow seeds in shallow soil in spring, directly in the flowering site. Autumn-sown seedlings need protection over winter but produce earlier-flowering plants.

POSSIBLE PROBLEMS Slugs may damage seedlings.

PLATYCODON

| summer | hardy | full sun | 23cm/9in | 30cm/12in |

Platycodon grandiflorum is a perennial member of the bell flower family. Because of the curious inflated form of its flowerbuds it is commonly called balloon flower. These 'balloons' open to become bells of blue or white. The compact species best for rock gardens is *P. g. mariesii*, with deep blue flowers 5cm/2in across. There are no named varieties.

GROWING Plant in late autumn or early spring in well-drained soil in a sunny position. Balloon flowers are slow to establish themselves and dislike disturbance. It is a good idea to mark the site so that the roots are not inadvertently damaged when top growth has died down.

PROPAGATION Divide mature (4-year-old) plants in spring and replant, handling the roots carefully. Raising from seed is more reliable. Sow seeds in spring in shallow drills in a nursery bed. Transplant to the flowering site when the seedlings are large enough to handle but before the fleshy roots have formed.

POSSIBLE PROBLEMS Generally trouble-free.

ORGANIC TIP

Alpines generally have little value in an organic garden, but the bell-shaped flowers of this plant will be sure to attract bees and other nectar-loving insects.

SPECIAL CARE TIP

Alpines rarely need any fertilizer or special feeding. Only feed plants if they look as if they have stopped growing completely, after a few years. The best way to feed is to give a light dusting or blood, fish and bone, which can be lightly watered in.

ARABIS

| spring | hardy | semi-shade | 23cm/9in | 60cm/24in |

Of the large number of species bearing the name, only one arabis, *A. albida* (syn. *A. caucasica*) is suitable for the rock garden. A perennial, it forms a cushion of grey-green, oval leaves covered in white flowers 1cm/½in wide from early spring to summer. The species is an invasive plant which cannot be allowed to range unchecked over the rock garden, but, in partnership with alyssum and aubrieta, can look wonderful scrambling over a dry wall or bank. Named varieties are recommended for the rock garden proper.

GROWING Plant in well-drained soil in autumn or spring. The stems can be pegged down for the sake of neatness; cut back hard after flowering to remove faded flower stems.

PROPAGATION Lift, divide and replant in autumn.

VARIETIES 'Flore-Pleno', double, white; 'Snowflake', large, single flowers, white; 'Corfe Castle', deep magenta.

POSSIBLE PROBLEMS Gall midge larvae on young growth; white blister, club root.

CERASTIUM

| summer | hardy | full sun | 7.5cm/3in | 60cm/24in |

Although the daisy-like white flowers are charming, cerastiums are chiefly valued for their dense, silvery foliage. The common name, snow-in-summer, is very apt, as these perennial plants form a thick white carpet over the ground. Some species are invasive, others nothing but weeds. Take care to obtain those recommended.

GROWING Plant in spring or early autumn in poor, well-drained soil in a sunny position. A south-facing bank is ideal. Protect the foliage from damp in winter with a pane of glass.

PROPAGATION Divide established plants in summer and replant immediately.

SPECIES *Cerastium tomentosum* (*above*)is pretty but invasive; the form *C. t. columnae* is neater and can be contained; *C. alpinum* can be recommended at 10cm/4in high, spreading only 23cm/9in and flowering all summer. A good late-flowering species is *C. pyrenaicum*, with tufted green leaves.

POSSIBLE PROBLEMS Generally trouble-free.

■ PLANTING TIP

Where there is no space for a rock garden proper, you can still grow trailing alpines such as arabis either by contructing small two-level plot or by making a scree bed as an edging to a border or path. The bed is paved to form a box with sides about 25cm/10in high and a concrete base filled with peat and sand.

■ PLANTING TIP

This is the ideal carpeting, or ground cover plant, as it will smother any weeds around it. Although it is an alpine, avoid planting in the rock garden as even the less invasive variety will spread too much to keep under control.

LEONTOPODIUM

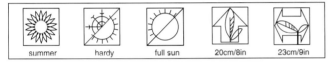

| summer | hardy | full sun | 20cm/8in | 23cm/9in |

Leontopodium alpinum, better known as edelweiss, is a perennial member of the daisy family which grows in alpine meadows throughout Europe. It forms attractive clumps with woolly, grey-green leaves and white 'flowers' (actually bracts) in summer.

GROWING Plant in spring in well-drained, preferably sandy soil, on an open sunny site.

PROPAGATION Edelweiss are easy to raise from seed. Sow in early spring in boxes of a potting compost/grit mixture and place in a cold frame. Prick off the seedlings into boxes when they are large enough to handle and then into individual pots. Keep in the cold frame until planting out the following spring.

VARIETIES The species is reliable. 'Mignon' is a good dwarf form at 10cm/4in high.

POSSIBLE PROBLEMS Generally trouble-free.

NIEREMBERGIA

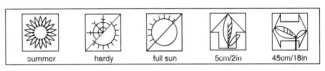

| summer | hardy | full sun | 5cm/2in | 45cm/18in |

Nierembergia repens is a member of the nightshade family, a perennial from South America which forms a mat of rooting stems. White flowers 2.5cm/1in wide with golden stamens are borne in mid summer. Sometimes the petals have a rosy tinge. There are no named varieties.

GROWING Plant in spring in moisture-retentive soil in a sunny position.

PROPAGATION Divide in spring and replant immediately.

POSSIBLE PROBLEMS Generally trouble-free.

■ SPECIAL CARE TIP

In the wild, alpines are protected by snow in winter. In damper winter conditions, protect plants with a small plastic or glass housing to keep off heavy

■ ORGANIC TIP

Weeding alpines in a rock garden can be a chore, as it is so fiddly. Keep down weeds by covering any soil between plants with coarse grit or ornamental stones.

SANTOLINA

summer	hardy	full sun	45cm/18in	45cm/18in

Clumps of cotton lavender, studded with button-shaped yellow flowers, add height to the miniature landscape of the rock garden and look splendid in sunny borders. The fern-like silver foliage of this dwarf shrub is aromatic.

GROWING Plant container-grown plants at any time when the weather is favourable, but preferably in spring or autumn. Remove flower stems when they have faded. Cut back hard in spring to keep the plants compact.

PROPAGATION Take half-ripe cuttings 5-7.5cm/2-3in long in summer and insert in a peat/sand mixture in a cold frame. Pot up the following spring and harden off before planting out in autumn.

SPECIES *S. chamaecyparissus* (syn. *S. incana*) forms a compact mound, lemon-yellow flowers; *S. rosmarinifolia* (syn. *S. virens, above*), taller at 60cm/24in, spreads to 90cm/3ft, emerald green thread-like leaves, bright yellow flowers.

POSSIBLE PROBLEMS Generally trouble-free.

JUNIPERUS

non-flowering	hardy	sun/semi-shade	60cm/24in	2m/6ft 6in

Juniper trees may be divided broadly into those that are columnar in form and those that are spreading, though there are variations. The leaves are usually needle-shaped when young, scale-like in maturity. They may be green, grey-green or blue; all are slow-growing. Some species bear fruits (berries or cones). Junipers make good focal points in a formal rock garden.

GROWING Plant seedlings in late spring, on well-drained soil in full sun or light shade.

PROPAGATION Take heeled cuttings 7.5cm/3in long in autumn and insert in a peat/sand mixture in a cold frame until rooted. Pot up individually and place outdoors or grow on in a nursery bed. Plant out after two years.

VARIETIES *Juniperus sabina* 'Tamariscifolia' (Spanish juniper); the bright green needle-like leaves release an aromatic oil if bruised; dense, prostrate habit, the stems building up in layers; prune to limit size. *J. communis* 'Compressa', dwarf form of the Irish juniper at 60cm/24in high, columnar, grey-blue foliage; best in groups of 3 or 5, no pruning. *J. virginiana* 'Globosa', dwarf rounded bush, 90cm × 90cm/3 × 3ft, pale green foliage, no pruning.

POSSIBLE PROBLEMS Scale insects; rust.

▦ PLANTING TIP

A sunny, well-drained site is essential for this low-growing shrub. The rock garden is the ideal place for it, but if it is planted in a border, keep it to the front, and ensure that the soil is not heavy or waterlogged. If necessary, dig in some gravel and compost before planting, to improve drainage conditions.

▦ PLANTING TIP

The compact size and columnar shape of this dwarf variety makes it ideal for patio or balcony containers, where it will provide all-year colour.

Alyssum

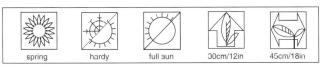

spring	hardy	full sun	30cm/12in	45cm/18in

Thanks to the brightness of its profuse yellow flowers, *Alyssum saxatile* (*above*) has an impact out of proportion to its diminutive size. This popular perennial, commonly known as gold-dust, is a shrubby plant with narrow, pointed, grey-green leaves. It carries its tiny blooms into the first weeks of summer. For a continuation of colour, plant with *A. argenteum*, which blooms all summer.

GROWING Plant between autumn and spring on light, free-draining soil. Over-rich soils are unsuitable. Cut back hard after flowering for sturdy growth and to keep the shape neat.

PROPAGATION Take 5cm/2in cuttings in early summer and insert in a peat/sand mixture in a cold frame until rooted. Pot up individually and grow on in the frame. Plant out the following spring.

VARIETIES 'Citrinum', sharp yellow; 'Compactum', neat, half the height of the species; 'Plenum' syn. 'Flore-Pleno', double golden-yellow flowers; 'Dudley Neville', dull gold.

POSSIBLE PROBLEMS Slugs may eat young plants; downy mildew on leaves.

Corydalis

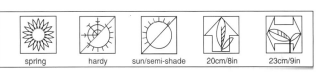

spring	hardy	sun/semi-shade	20cm/8in	23cm/9in

Corydalis lutea is the common yellow fumitory often found growing wild on old walls. More garden-worthy are *C. cheilanthifolia* (*above*) and *C. cashmeriana*. The former shares with its wild cousin a tendency to self-seed, which in the less formal settings which it suits may not be a problem. The fern-like foliage is slightly bronzed, arranged in tufts from which rise dense racemes of long-lasting yellow flowers. There are no named varieties. The species *C. cashmeriana* is a fussier plant, requiring cool, humid conditions, but its beautiful blue flowers make it well worth growing in areas where the climate is suitable.

GROWING Plant in spring on any good garden soil. *C. cashmeriana* must have cool, peat, totally lime-free soil.

PROPAGATION Self-sown seedlings of *C. cheilanthifolia* do well. Corydalis may be increased by careful division of the delicate tubers in early autumn. Replant immediately.

POSSIBLE PROBLEMS Generally trouble-free.

▌ PLANTING TIP

With its tiny, bright flowers, this is the ideal plant where space is limited – plant in hanging baskets, tubs or containers. Some forms bloom all summer.

▌ SPECIAL CARE TIP

The Himalayan version of this plant may prove difficult to grow as it likes a cool situation in a totally peat soil. Plant in a shady corner of the rockery, or on a shaded wall, in a specially made 'pocket' filled with peat.

PRIMULA

| spring | hardy | semi-shade | 10cm/4in | 15cm/6in |

For a cool, semi-shaded position, there are few alpine plants to better the diminutive species primulas. With primrose-like flowers in subtle shades of pink and lilac as well as white, these hardy perennials also look attractive in old stone troughs.

GROWING Plant between autumn and spring in well-drained, humus-rich, gritty soil. Species vary in their precise requirements.

PROPAGATION Divide after flowering and replant immediately. *Primula auricula* may be raised from 2.5cm/1in cuttings taken in summer.

SPECIES *P. frondosa* (*above*), rosette of grey-green leaves, each flower stem bearing up to 30 rose-pink flowers, needs a moist position; *P. clarkei*, only 5cm/2in high, bright pink flowers 1cm/⅜in across appear while the pale green leaves are unfolding; *P. reidii*, unusual bell-shaped flowers, white, fragrant, late spring; *P.r.* 'Williamsii' bears blue, more fragrant flowers; *P. auricula*, 15cm/6in high, umbels of long-lived yellow or purple flowers. Several fine varieties available including 'The Mikado', dark red, and 'Blue Fire'. *P. juliae*, low-growing, reddish-purple flowers; numerous excellent varieties including 'Snow Cushion', white, dwarf; 'Wanda', wine-red, flowers mid-winter; 'Our Pat', double dark crimson flowers.

POSSIBLE PROBLEMS Virus diseases, grey mould, rot.

ARMERIA

| summer | hardy | full sun | 15cm/6in | 30cm/12in |

Armeria maritima or sea thrift (*above*) is a familiar wild plant of coastal areas from which a number of attractive garden varieties have been developed. The perennial plants make neat hummocks and the long-lasting flower-heads – like pinks in form and usually pink in colour – are carried high on slender stems. The species *A. caespitosa*, by contrast, bears almost stemless flowers.

GROWING Plant between autumn and spring in well-drained soil in full sun. Snip off flower-heads as they fade.

PROPAGATION Lift, divide and replant in spring.

VARIETIES *A. maritima*: 'Alba', white; 'Vindictive', deep rose-red; 'Merlin', deep pink. *A. caespitosa*: 'Bevan's Variety', deep pink.

POSSIBLE PROBLEMS Rust.

■ SPECIAL CARE TIP

Alpine primulas are best given a layer of grit around their collars to prevent water collecting in the rosettes. As with other rosette-forming alpines, they should be protected from too much rain in winter by means of mini-cloches.

■ PLANTING TIP

An ideal sun-loving plant for the small rock garden. It will cope with a windy site even in seaside gardens. It can also be grown at the edge of tubs or between paving stones, where it will produce attractive hummocks of spiky, grass-like leaves.

ERINUS

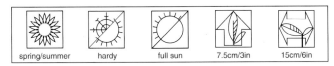

spring/summer	hardy	full sun	7.5cm/3in	15cm/6in

Erinus alpinus is one of those cheerful perennial plants that commends itself to the gardener by giving great rewards in return for almost no attention. Once established in a sunny position on the rock garden or a dry wall, it flowers for weeks, self-seeds freely to produce new plants after its short life is done, and as an evergreen gives year-round cover. The tiny, star-shaped flowers are bright pink.

GROWING Plant out seedlings in spring, in well-drained, poor soil in a sunny position. Trim lightly after flowering.

PROPAGATION Scatter the seed in spring where it is to grow. Most named forms come true.

VARIETIES 'Albus', white; 'Dr Hanaele', crimson; 'Mrs Charles Boyle', coral pink.

POSSIBLE PROBLEMS Generally trouble-free.

HELIANTHEMUM

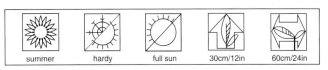

summer	hardy	full sun	30cm/12in	60cm/24in

There are several species of helianthemum available, but it is *H. nummularium* which has earned the name rock rose. This perennial forms dense mounds of small green or grey leaves and bears numerous yellow saucer-shaped flowers 2.5cm/1in across in early summer. The petals are papery, like those of poppies. *H. alpestre* is a more compact species, *H. apenninum* rather larger.

GROWING Plant in autumn or spring in light, well-drained soil. The rock rose should be cut right back after flowering to keep it neat; all species respond to trimming by flowering a second time in autumn.

PROPAGATION Take 2.5cm/1in cuttings of non-flowering side shoots in mid summer. Place in pots of a peat/sand mixture in a cold frame until rooted. Pot up individually in potting compost and overwinter in the frame. Pinch out the growing tips. Plant out in spring.

VARIETIES *H. nummularium*: 'Ben Heckla', copper; 'Ben Afflick', orange and buff; 'Wisley Pink' *(above)*, rose-pink; 'Cerise Queen', rose-red; 'The Bride', white; 'Beech Park Scarlet', red. *H. apenninum*: 'Roseum', rose red. *H. alpestre*: 'Serpyllifolium', very low growing at 5-7.5cm/2-3in.

POSSIBLE PROBLEMS In hot conditions powdery mildew may occur.

▨ SPECIAL CARE TIP

Ideal for planting in a bare wall, where it will give all-year-round cover. Wrap the roots in a piece of old turf soaked in water, and push firmly into a prepared hole.

▨ PLANTING TIP

Ideal for a site where you want quick growth and colour, this plant will provide a multitude of attractive yellow flowers. It is excellent for dry walls.

GENTIANA

| autumn | hardy | semi-shade | 15cm/6in | 30cm/12in |

LEWISIA

| spring/summer | hardy | full sun | 23cm/9in | 15cm/6in |

A number of gentians are in cultivation, with widely varying requirements and flowering times. Broadly speaking, these perennials are divided into European species, which are spring-flowering, and the Asiatic species described here which flower in the autumn. The flowers are large, trumpet-shaped and of a uniquely intense blue. They are among the most distinguished alpine plants.

GROWING Plant out in spring, in deep soil previously enriched with leaf-mould or peat. Do not let the soil dry out. Always check the lime-tolerance of individual species.

PROPAGATION Lift, divide and replant in spring. All species may be raised from cuttings taken from the basal shoots in spring and treated as for helianthemums.

SPECIES *Gentiana sino-ornata (above)*, easy to grow in acid soil, abundant 5cm/2in long deep blue flowers striped purplish blue, a much admired species; *G. farreri*, lime-tolerant, clear light blue flowers with white throats from late summer; *G. × 'Stevenagensis'*, strong-growing prostrate hybrid, deep purple blue, late summer.

POSSIBLE PROBLEMS Root rot on poorly drained soil.

Lewisias are semi-succulent perennials. Those described here are reliably hardy, but there are other fine species which need the protection of an alpine house. Native to North America, the pink flowers rise on erect stems from rosette-forming fleshy mid-green leaves. *Lewisia cotyledon* is a variable species which has given rise to many named forms of varying colours, bearing masses of daisy-like flowers in late spring.

GROWING Plant in spring, placing the rosettes at an angle to prevent water collecting in the centre. Set in rich, gritty soil and place a collar of gravel around the neck of the plants to assist drainage. Water regularly, but give less in the winter.

PROPAGATION Remove offsets in summer and insert in boxes of a sand/peat mixture in a cold frame until rooted. Pot up individually in compost, overwinter in the frame and plant out in spring.

VARIETIES *L. c. heckneri (above)*, toothed leaves, deep pink striped flowers; *L. c. howelli*, narrow leaves, rose-pink flowers. Many good named hybrids include 'George Henley', terracotta; 'Sunset Strain', mixed colours, including orange and yellow.

POSSIBLE PROBLEMS Excessive moisture causes collar rot.

▦ PLANTING TIP

The ideal plant if you have a moist, peaty soil: if not, you will need to provide a special peat-filled pocket in the rock garden and ensure that it does not dry out.

▦ SPECIAL CARE TIP

Another alpine which needs winter protection from rain, as water collects in the rosettes and causes rot. A sheet of glass, supported on wire legs, will do the trick.

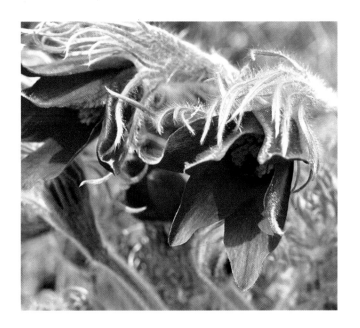

PULSATILLA

spring

hardy

full sun

30cm/12in

38cm/15in

Closely related to anemones, pulsatillas are perennials native to European mountain regions. Two species are suitable for rock gardens. *P. vulgaris* is known as the pasque flower. It is easy to grow and bears large purple flowers surrounded by a frill of fine, hairy leaves. The foliage is delicate and fern-like. *P. alpina* bears long-lasting white flowers flushed blue on the outside, followed by fluffy silver seedheads. Once established, both species are long-lived.

GROWING Plant in autumn in an open, sunny site on alkaline, free-draining soil. Do not disturb the plants thereafter.

PROPAGATION Sow fresh seed in summer in trays of seed compost in a cold frame. When the seedlings are large enough to handle, prick off into boxes and overwinter in the frame. Pot up individually when new leaves appear in spring. Water well as the plants develop and plant out in autumn.

VARIETIES *P. vulgaris*: 'Rubra' *(above)*, glowing red; 'Budapest', reddish-purple. *P. alpina*: 'Sulphurea', sharp yellow flowers last until mid summer.

POSSIBLE PROBLEMS Generally trouble-free.

SAXIFRAGA

spring

hardy

semi-shade

5cm/2in

38cm/15in

The saxifrage family is large and complex, but all of its members are suitable for the rock garden. Certain types have rosettes of silvery or grey-green leaves that grow in hummocks or form mats; others are known as moss saxifrage because of the appearance of their densely packed leaves. The flowers may be star- or saucer-shaped, yellow, white, pink or red and are very freely borne. The species described here is the best-known mossy type, *S. moschata*.

GROWING Plant out in autumn or spring in any good garden soil in a shady site.

PROPAGATION After flowering, lift, divide and replant immediately. Alternatively, detach non-flowering rosettes in early summer, place in pans of a peat/sand mixture in a cold frame and water generously. Thereafter water sparingly until the following spring; water well over the summer, pot up individually in the autumn and plant out the following spring.

VARIETIES 'Dubarry' *(above)*, 15cm/6in high, deep red flowers; 'Peter Pan', hybrid, pink flowers on red stems, bright green leaves; 'Cloth of Gold', bright yellow leaves, white flowers.

POSSIBLE PROBLEMS Grubs and root aphids may attack the roots.

▊ SPECIAL CARE TIP

This plant, with its beautiful violet flowers, thrives in full sun and in alkaline soil, but does not like to be disturbed after being established.

Its native habitat is mountainous, so its ideal position is in a rockery. Failing that, plant in an open position in a well-drained border.

▊ PLANTING TIP

As with all rock plants, it is important to ensure that they have an open, sunny site well away from surface-rooting trees such as poplars or silver birch. If

the garden is small, or trees are established, it may be necessary to grow the plants in containers, raised above the ground and sited away from the trees.

ERODIUM

| summer | hardy | full sun | 2.5cm/1in | 23cm/9in |

Erodiums bear a close resemblance to their cousins the true geraniums or cranesbills. These are compact perennials, however, forming tufts or mats of small mid-green leaves studded with pink, white, or yellow flowers. They bloom throughout the summer.

GROWING Plant in spring in a sunny, sheltered position on well-drained, poor soil, preferably on the limy side.

PROPAGATION Take 5cm/2in basal cuttings in spring and insert in a peat/sand mixture in a cold frame. Plant out in the autumn or – after overwintering in the cold frame – the following spring. *E. chamaedryoides* must be increased by root cuttings taken in early spring. Treat as basal cuttings, potting them up when 3-4 leaves have formed, and plant out in the spring.

SPECIES *E. chrysanthum*, reaches 15cm/6in, silvery fern-like-leaves, sprays of acid yellow flowers; *E. chamaedryoides*, mat-forming, pink-veined white flowers; the variety 'Roseum' *(above)* bears clear pink flowers in late spring; *E. corsicum*, pink flowers in late spring, downy, soft leaves need protection from winter damp.

POSSIBLE PROBLEMS Generally trouble-free.

GERANIUM

| summer | hardy | sun/semi-shade | 12.5cm/5in | 45cm/18in |

The large group of true geraniums or cranesbills includes several species indispensable to the rock garden. Flowers may be pink, lilac or white and the attractive leaves form dense ground cover.

GROWING Plant in autumn or spring in well-drained soil in sun or partial shade. After flowering, cut back stems to ground level to keep the shape neat and encourage a second flush of flowers.

PROPAGATION Lift, divide and replant between autumn and spring.

SPECIES *G. dalmaticum (above)* forms cushions of foliage flushed orange in the autumn, pale pink flowers; *G.* × 'Ballerina', strong-growing hybrid, grey-green leaves, pink flowers veined red; *G. napuligerum*, slow-growing, suitable for a rocky bank, pink flowers – 'Album' is a white variety; *G. pylzowianum*, best ground cover plant for rock gardens, 7.5cm/3in high, relatively few pink flowers; *G. renardii*, clump-forming, with large lavender flowers veined purple; *G. subcaulescens*, bright crimson flowers in profusion from spring to autumn – the hybrid 'Russell Prichard' makes excellent ground cover with grey-green leaves and large, rich pink flowers.

POSSIBLE PROBLEMS Slugs eat young plants; rust on leaves.

▦ SPECIAL CARE TIP

This plant is native to the Mediterranean, so it is obviously a sun lover, well suited to a sunny, open position in the rock garden. Avoid too rich or acid soil – ideally the soil should be on the poor side – and make sure it is well drained.

▦ ORGANIC TIP

Deter slugs by mulching young plants with pine bark. You can also sink a small container into the ground and fill it with beer; the slugs fall in and drown.

SAPONARIA

| summer | hardy | sun/semi-shade | 7.5cm/3in | 30cm/12in |

The common name of *Saponaria officinalis* – soapwort – gives the hint to its former use as a cleansing herb (the leaves produce a lather in water). This species is too large and invasive for the rock garden, however; *S. ocymoides (above)* is the one to choose, a vigorous perennial which forms trailing mats of small green leaves. Throughout the summer it bears a profusion of bright pink flowers.

GROWING Plant between autumn and spring in good garden soil in sun or partial shade. Cut back after flowering to encourage further blooms and cut back hard in late autumn.

PROPAGATION Divide and replant the roots or detach underground runners and replant between autumn and spring.

VARIETIES 'Compacta', slow-growing, neat habit; 'Rubra Compacta', rich pink flowers.

POSSIBLE PROBLEMS Generally trouble-free.

SILENE

| summer | hardy | full sun | 2.5-15cm/1-6in | 30cm/12in |

Silenes, members of the carnation family, are commonly known as campions. Two perennial species are suitable for the rock garden; both are spreading plants bearing delicate pink flowers throughout the summer.

GROWING Plant in autumn or spring in well-drained soil on a sunny site.

PROPAGATION Take 4cm/1½in cuttings of healthy outer shoots in summer. Place in a peat/sand mixture in a cold frame until rooted. Pot up individually in compost, overwinter in the frame and plant out the following autumn. Silenes resent root disturbance.

SPECIES *S. acaulis* (moss campion or cushion pink, *above*), prostrate, tightly packed tiny leaves, may be slow to flower; *S. schafta*, easy to grow, reaches 15cm/6in high, deep pink flowers; tolerates some shade.

POSSIBLE PROBLEMS Generally trouble-free.

■ PLANTING TIP

Rock gardens should always be open and in full sun, well away from any overhanging trees – dripping trees will soon destroy your plants.

However, saponaria will tolerate partial shade, or dappled sunlight. Plant in a container in a small garden or in the partial shade of a wall.

■ PLANTING TIP

Prostrate alpines look charming planted in cracks in patios or in crazy paving, or between slabs of a path. Fill the gaps with a peat mixture before planting.

IBERIS

summer	hardy	full sun	23cm/9in	60cm/24in

There are three species of sub-shrubby perennial iberis, commonly called candytuft, suitable for the rock garden. All have dark green narrow leaves and bear numerous heads of densely packed flowers of white or lilac over a long period. As they are tolerant of polluted atmospheres iberis are a good choice for town gardens.

GROWING Plant between autumn and spring in any well-drained garden soil. They thrive on poor soils.

PROPAGATION Take 5cm/2in softwood cuttings of non-flowering shoots in summer. Place in a cold frame in a peat/sand mixture until rooted. Pot up individually and overwinter in the frame, setting out the young plants the following spring.

SPECIES *Iberis gibraltarica*, semi-evergreen, not fully hardy but self-seeds freely, lilac flowers in spring; *I. saxatilis*, only 7.5cm/3in high, spread 30cm/12in, neat form, white flowers spring to summer; *I. sempervirens*, variable in form. The variety 'Little Gem' *(above)*, with white flowers, is neat at 10cm/4in high, spread 23cm/9in; 'Snowflake' has pure white flowers and is more spreading in habit.

POSSIBLE PROBLEMS Flea beetles may puncture the leaves.

SISYRINCHIUM

spring/summer	hardy	full sun	23cm/9in	15cm/6in

Sisyrinchiums are handsome members of the iris family. Their erect flower spikes, clothed with star-shaped flowers of violet, blue or yellow, are useful for bringing height to a rock garden design. The fresh green leaves are long and narrow. Different species are in flower from spring through to autumn.

GROWING Plant between spring and autumn on well-drained soil into which plenty of peat or leaf-mould has been incorporated. Choose a site where the plants will not be disturbed. In autumn remove the dead leaves and stems.

PROPAGATION Species come true from seeds, which will germinate where they fall if the ground is undisturbed. Alternatively lift, divide, and replant in autumn or spring.

SPECIES *S. striatum (above)*, reaches 45cm/18in, innumerable creamy-yellow flowers in mid summer; *S. angustifolium*, clumps of grassy leaves, violet flowers right through summer; *S. grandiflorum*, bell-shaped purple flowers in early spring; plant in close groups for best effect.

POSSIBLE PROBLEMS Generally trouble-free.

▓ PLANTING TIP

The perfect plant for poor soil or a problem site such as a hot, dry wall. This vigorous, trailing plant also thrives in a rock garden or on a dry, sunny bank.

▓ SPECIAL CARE TIP

These flowers, members of the iris family, are native to Bermuda and Chile, so they need full sun and a sheltered position. In cooler areas of the world, they are better grown in containers. They can then be kept in a conservatory or greenhouse and brought out when the temperature is high enough.

SOLDANELLA

| spring | hardy | full sun | 7.5cm/3in | 20cm/8in |

Soldanellas are members of the primula family. They bear nodding, pale lilac flowers with fringed petals. Rounded mid-green leaves cluster at the foot of the erect stems. Native to European alpine meadows, these modest flowers suit informal planting schemes.

GROWING Plant in autumn or early summer in well-drained soil. A sunny position is preferred but some shade is tolerated. Place a collar of grit around each plant to assist drainage.

PROPAGATION Lift and divide the plants after flowering. Either replant in the permanent positions straight away or pot up in a compost/peat mixture and overwinter in a cold frame, planting out the following spring.

SPECIES *S. alpina (above)*, mat-forming foliage, lavender flowers; *S. montana*, larger, strong-growing species with bell-shaped flowers; *S. minima*, smallest at 5cm/2in high, best choice for ground cover, delicate lilac flowers; *S. villosa*, slightly hairy leaves, lavender flowers tinted deep blue.

POSSIBLE PROBLEMS Slugs may eat young plants.

AETHIONEMA

| spring | hardy | sun | 15cm/6in | 37cm/15in |

Aethionemas are evergreen perennials which will respond to a position in the sun with a long-lived display of beautiful pink or white flowers, the thick mat of leaves persisting through the winter.

GROWING Plant in spring in well-drained soil that is not too rich. Dead-head regularly and there may be a second flush of flowers.

PROPAGATION Plants may self-seed, but can be raised from non-flowering softwood cuttings taken in summer. Insert in a peat/sand mixture in a cold frame until rooted. Pot up individually, overwinter in the frame and plant out the following spring.

SPECIES A. × 'Warley Rose' *(above)*, the most popular hybrid, with small grey-green pointed leaves, rose-pink flowers; *A. grandiflorum*, height and spread 45cm/18in, deep pink flowerheads 7.5cm/3in long; *A. pulchellum*, 20cm/8in high, numerous rich pink flowers; *A. iberideum*, blue-green leaves, profuse white flowers.

POSSIBLE PROBLEMS Generally trouble-free.

▧ SPECIAL CARE TIP

Soldanellas are native to the Alps and Pyrenees, so conditions must be similar. The ideal situation is either in a coolish rock garden – possibly with some shade – or in a peat garden. You must protect plants against excessive moisture in winter with a mini-cloche or piece of glass.

▧ SPECIAL CARE TIP

This beautiful plant is no trouble given a well-drained site with lime-free soil. If necessary, provide a container and fill with a special peat mixture.

SHRUBS

Shrubs give the garden an established appearance, forming the main framework of most planting schemes around which perennials, annuals and bulbs are grouped.

As in all garden schemes, the principle behind choosing and siting shrubs is balance, for example between evergreen and deciduous species. Although all the shrubs in this chapter have been selected for their flowers, there is no denying the importance of foliage. An equally important factor is the season of interest. In a large garden with numerous shrubs you can include some specially for each season; in a smaller space with room for only two or three, it is a good idea to go for those that have something to offer all year, or at least at more than one time. *Mahonia aquifolium* 'Atropurpurea', for example, is an evergreen which flowers in mid winter, bears berries in spring and summer, and whose foliage turns a lovely red in autumn. Other worthwhile evergreens include camellia, *Ceanothus impressus*,

choisya, *Erica carnea*, pieris and many rhododendrons.

Spring-flowering shrubs are particularly useful at a time when most of the colour in the garden is at ground level, provided by swathes of bulbs. Try to limit the number of yellow-flowering spring shrubs, as there is likely to be a strong yellow element anyway at this time. For white, pink and red, try *Magnolia stellata*, rhododendrons and azaleas, enkianthus, choisya, pieris and chaenomeles.

It is a characteristic of the modern border that shrubs are included to add height and texture to the display. In summer, old roses, potentillas, fuchsias and spiraeas combine particularly well with other plants. Climbers at the back of the border complete the picture, whether against a fine old wall or a wooden fence. It is difficult to make a choice between such delectable species as clematis, climbing roses and honeysuckles (*Lonicera* species). Because many honeysuckles are fragrant they are often planted against the wall of the house, next to a window so that the scent will waft inside. Other scented shrubs are philadelphus, choisya, lavender and lilac.

Increasing emphasis on winter colour in the garden has put the focus on shrubs such as *Chimonanthus praecox* (winter sweet) and *Jasminum nudiflorum* (winter-flowering jasmine), two yellow-flowering species. The viburnums *V. tinus* and *V. farreri* both bear white flowers during the winter; consider too the little-known honeysuckle *Lonicera × purpusii*, which bears small, scented, cream flowers for many weeks in the middle of winter. For cold-weather glamour, nothing can outclass the camellia, with its huge red, pink or white flowers.

PLANTING SHRUBS Like trees, shrubs are sold bare-rooted, with a ball of soil around the roots, or in containers. Those in containers can be planted at any time of year as long as the soil is not allowed to dry out. Bare-rooted and balled-root shrubs should be planted between autumn and spring (see individual entries for variations). Cut off any damaged roots from bare-rooted specimens. Plants in

containers should be well-watered before planting.

1 Take out a planting hole to a depth such that the old soil mark on the stem, or, on a container-grown plant, the base of the stem, will be level with the soil. Fork over the soil at the bottom of the hole.

2 Mix the soil from the hole with half its volume of well-rotted compost, manure or peat.

3 Remove the plant from the container and place it in the hole. Do not remove sacking from a balled-root shrub until you have placed it in the hole. Holding the shrub by its stem, replace the soil in the hole, tread it down and top up with more soil. Tread the soil down again and water in generously.

4 When planting a bare-rooted shrub, spread the roots out and lift the shrub up and down a few times to make sure the soil settles around them.

PLANTING CLIMBERS Some climbers are self-clinging and need no supports; where supports are required, it is

The summer-flowering Deutzia × rosea is a rewarding shrub which, when pruned effectively, will produce an abundance of blossom.

essential to put them securely in place before planting. Wide-gauge plastic netting is suitable for a wide range of plants and soft enough not to damage delicate stems. A system of horizontal wires is efficient and inconspicuous. Whichever you use, mount the mesh or wires on battens to keep them at least 2.5cm/1in clear of the wall so that air can circulate. Start training the climber to the supports as soon as its tendrils become long enough to encourage it to grow in the desired direction.

When planting, follow the instructions for shrubs, but remember that because soil at the foot of a wall or fence is relatively dry, you need to give it a good soaking the day before planting and keep it moist afterwards. Do not set the plant too close to the wall or it will not benefit from rain – 30cm/12in is the correct distance.

FORSYTHIA

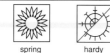

| spring | hardy | sun/semi-shade | 2.4m/8ft | 2.1m/7ft |

Forsythia is an easily grown shrub whose brilliant yellow flowers appear before the foliage. It is very successful in town gardens. *Forsythia suspensa* is suitable as a wall shrub for any aspect, while *F. × intermedia* is the best choice for hedging.

GROWING Plant from autumn to spring in any moderately fertile soil in sun or partial shade. *F. × intermedia* grown as a hedge should be planted in autumn. Set 45cm/18in high plants the 45cm/18in apart. Cut back all shoots by one-third after planting. Pinch out the growing tips at 15cm/6in. Clip established hedges lightly in spring after flowering. Prune all species in spring to neaten and to clear damaged wood.

PROPAGATION Take 30cm/12in cuttings of the current season's growth in autumn and insert in a nursery bed outdoors for planting out one year later. The drooping branches of *F. suspensa* sometimes take root where they touch the ground. Separate the rooted layers in autumn and treat as cuttings.

SPECIES *F. × intermedia (above)*, hybrid form bearing abundant flowers on stiff branches. 'Spectabilis' is the most common variety, compact in shape with vivid flowers; *F. suspensa*, rambling habit, may exceed 3 x 3m/10 x 10ft on a wall. *F. s. sieboldii* has trailing stems.

POSSIBLE PROBLEMS Birds eat flowerbuds; honey fungus can kill plants.

■ PLANTING TIP

Can be planted as informal hedging and clipped to keep in shape. Prune flowering shoots immediately after flowering to control the growth.

CYTISUS

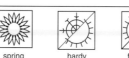

| spring | hardy | full sun | 12.5m/5ft | 1.5m/5ft |

Brooms are handsome shrubs, including both deciduous and evergreen species. All flower profusely in spring and early summer, with small cream, yellow, red or multi-coloured blooms of the pea-flower form. They are short-lived (particularly on limy soils) but easily propagated plants.

GROWING Set out young pot-grown plants in autumn or spring in well-drained, rather poor soil. Full sun is important. Prune species which flower on the previous season's shoots directly after flowering – remove two-thirds of all growth. Cut back those which flower on the current season's shoots just before flowering if necessary to maintain a compact shape.

PROPAGATION Raise species from seed sown in spring in pans in a cold frame. Pot on when the seedlings are large enough to handle and set outdoors. Plant out in the autumn. Raise named varieties from 10cm/4in cuttings taken in early autumn (see page 17).

SPECIES *Cytisus × praecox* (Warminster broom, *above*), hybrid, arching stems covered with pale yellow flowers; 'Allgold' has acid-yellow blooms. *C. scoparius* (common broom), early summer-flowering, upright habit. Good named varieties include 'Burkwoodii', crimson; 'Cornish Cream', cream and white, 'Goldfinch', purple, red and yellow.

POSSIBLE PROBLEMS Stems may be disfigured by gall mites.

■ PLANTING TIP

A good shrub for difficult positions: it will tolerate a hot, dry spot (such as against a sunny wall) that would kill off more tender shrubs.

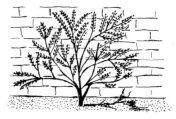

CHIMONANTHUS

winter	hardy	full sun	3m/10ft	2.4m/8ft

Chimonanthus praecox, the winter sweet, bears its heavily scented cup-shaped flowers of yellow and purple in the middle of winter on bare twigs. When the leaves appear they are like those of the willow family.

GROWING Set out young plants from autumn to spring in reasonably fertile soil, preferably with the protection of a sunny wall. If trained against a wall, prune hard in spring, cutting flowered shoots right back almost to the base. Those grown as bushes should be pruned after flowering to remove old and overcrowded branches.

PROPAGATION Raise from seed sown in a cold frame in autumn. Pot on when the seedling are large enough to handle and set oudoors. Plant in nursery rows in the autumn and into the permanent site 3 years later. Plants take at least 5 years to reach flowering size. Alternatively, long shoots may be layered *(see page 17)* in the autumn.

VARIETIES The species is sturdy and reliable. Named varieties include 'Lutens', all-yellow flowers, slow to reach maturity; 'Grandiflorus', larger flowers but less fragrant.

POSSIBLE PROBLEMS Generally trouble-free.

JASMINUM

winter	hardy	sun/shade	3m/10ft	2.4m/8ft

The winter-flowering jasmine, *Jasminum nudiflorum*, is a rambler which will bear its bright yellow flowers in almost any situation except one where the buds might be nipped by cold winds. The flowers appear in the axils of the previous season's leaves and are excellent for cutting. There are no named varieties.

GROWING Plant from autumn to spring in any well-drained soil, against a wall or where the plant can clamber over a bank. Provide supports as the branches will need tying in regularly. Prune in early spring: cut out old, weak stems and cut back flowered side shoots to within 7.5cm/3in of the base.

PROPAGATION Layer in autumn *(see page 17)* or take 7.5cm/3in cuttings of semi-ripe wood in late summer. Cut just below a node and place in a peat/sand mixture. Overwinter at 7-10°C/45-50°F. Pot up when rooted and plant out in the autumn.

POSSIBLE PROBLEMS Mealy bugs on soft shoots.

■ CUT FLOWER TIP

A must for the winter garden – its pretty yellow or lilac flowers will brighten up dark, winter days. The bare, flowering branches will also make very elegant indoor arrangements, and the delicate flowers will scent the whole house with their superb perfume.

■ PLANTING TIP

Generously spangled with yellow blooms that are produced continuously, this climber will help soften the bare walls of a house, or a patio, when there is little else of colour in the garden. Give it a fence, trellis or netting to cling to, which will also provide protection from strong winds.

SENECIO

| summer | half hardy | full sun | 1.2m/4ft | 1.8m/6ft |

The best shrubby senecio for most gardens is *Senecio* × 'Sunshine' *(above)*, sometimes inaccurately listed as *S. greyi* or *S. laxifolius*. Well-suited to coastal gardens, this evergreen has leaves of a beautiful silvery-grey. Though they turn green as the season progresses, the undersides remain silver. Clusters of daisy-like yellow flowers appear in early summer. It is not fully hardy in very severe winters.

GROWING Plant between autumn and spring in free-draining soil. Remove faded flowerheads as soon as you notice them. The minimum amount of pruning is required – simply remove dead or damaged wood in spring.

PROPAGATION Take 7.5cm/3in semi-ripe cuttings of side shoots in late summer. Place in a peat/sand mixture in a cold frame. Transfer the rooted cuttings to a nursery bed in spring or pot up individually and set outdoors. Plant out the following autumn.

POSSIBLE PROBLEMS Aphids.

THUNBERGIA

| summer | tender | full sun | 3m/10ft | 45cm/18in |

Native to South Africa, *Thunbergia alata* or black-eyed susan is a twining perennial grown as an annual in less favoured climates. It bears numerous funnel-shaped flowers of deep yellow with a black centre. Black-eyed susan can be grown on a sunny patio in a large pot, trained up a wigwam of canes which it will quickly obscure.

GROWING A position in full sun is essential, with fertile, moist soil. Plant against a wall, fence or post with the support of strings, wires or netting. Water in dry spells and discard after flowering.

PROPAGATION Sow seeds under glass in spring in small individual pots. Harden off and do not plant out until night temperatures exceed 10°C/50°F.

VARIETIES 'Susie', hardier than the species, profusion of yellow, orange and white flowers; 'Alba', white with black eye.

POSSIBLE PROBLEMS Generally trouble-free.

■ CUT FLOWER TIP

The beautiful yellow flowers are a marvellous source of cut flowers; they are also a good source of nectar for butterflies, so be sure to leave some.

■ PLANTING TIP

Remember to prepare the soil well when planting a climber against a wall, as this is likely to be a very dry spot. Make sure the soil is enriched with well-rotted manure or compost, and after planting, fork in some general fertilizer such as fish, blood and bone. Water well and mulch with compost to conserve moisture.

FREMONTIA

| summer | tender | full sun | 4m/12ft | 2.4m/8ft |

There are two species of fremontias but only one in general cultivation. *Fremontia californica*, as its name suggests, is a native of California (and Mexico). This deciduous shrub, though not a climber, is best grown against a warm sunny wall for protection as it is slightly tender. It should be trained against a trellis. Fabulous cup-shaped waxy yellow flowers, 5cm/2in across, are borne from late spring right through to early autumn.

GROWING Plant container-grown fremontias in autumn or spring in well-drained, sandy soil in full sun. Tie the trunk and main branches into the trellis. No pruning is necessary, but if any shoots are damaged by frost they should be removed in spring.

PROPAGATION Raise from seed sown in pots at 16°C/61°F in spring. Prick off the seedlings into individual pots of compost when they are large enough to handle. Pot on to larger pots (15cm/6in) and plant out the following spring.

VARIETIES *F.* × 'California Glory' *(above)* is a hybrid which is hardier than its parents.

POSSIBLE PROBLEMS Generally trouble-free.

POTENTILLA

| summer | hardy | full sun | 1.5m/5ft | 1.5m/5ft |

The shrubby cinquefoil, *Potentilla fruticosa*, is a perfect subject for low-maintenance gardens. Totally hardy and requiring virtually no attention if given the correct conditions, it produces five-petalled flowers of yellow, white or orange for the whole summer. There are a number of low-growing varieties which are suitable for ground cover.

GROWING Plant between autumn and spring in light, well-drained soil in full sun. Fewer flowers will be produced in partial shade. To maintain bushy growth, remove old or weak stems at ground level. Cut off the tips of flowering shoots after the blooms have faded. No other pruning is necessary.

PROPAGATION Take 7.5cm/3in half-ripe cuttings with a heel in autumn and place in a peat/sand mixture in a cold frame. Place the rooted cuttings in a nursery bed in spring and transfer to the final positions in the autumn of the following year.

VARIETIES 'Farreri', very delicate foliage, bright yellow flowers; 'Tangerine' *(above)*, low-growing, scarlet in bud, opening to orange, or yellow if in full sun; 'Mandschurica', only 30 × 90cm/1 × 3ft, silver leaves, purple stems, white flowers.

POSSIBLE PROBLEMS Generally trouble-free.

■ SPECIAL CARE TIP

This tender plant, native to California and Mexico, is only suitable for warm, sunny, sheltered gardens where it can be grown against a wall. In colder areas, it might be better off in a greenhouse or conservatory where it can be trained up a trellis.

■ PLANTING TIP

This shrub can be planted as an informal hedge. Simply remove flower shoots and old stems after flowers have faded. It flowers all summer.

PHILADELPHUS

summer	hardy	full sun	2.7m/9ft	2m/6ft6in

White-flowered shrubs are an important element in gardens and the philadelphus or mock orange is a popular choice, not only for the attraction of its abundant blooms but also because of its delicious scent. The species and hybrids vary in size and habit, but all are summer-flowering and have mid-green oval leaves.

GROWING Plant between autumn and spring in fertile well-drained soil, preferably in full sun. The exception is the golden-leaved *Philadelphus coronarius* 'Aureus', which prefers semi-shade to retain foliage colour. Prune after flowering by cutting back flowered shoots to a developing shoot which will flower the following year. Cut weak growths right back.

PROPAGATION Take 10cm/4in half-ripe cuttings in summer and place in a peat/sand mixture in a cold frame. Transfer the rooted cuttings to a nursery bed the following spring and plant out in the autumn.

SPECIES *P. coronarius*, vigorous grower, good on dry soils; *P. microphyllus*, neat at 60 × 60cm/24 × 24in, suitable for rock gardens. Many good garden hybrids are available. Try 'Manteau d'Hermine' *(above)*, 90cm/3ft high, double, creamy flowers; 'Belle Etoile', 1.5m/5ft, intensely fragrant white flowers flushed red in the centre; 'Virginal', 2.4m/8ft, double, white flowers.

POSSIBLE PROBLEMS Leaf spot.

■ ORGANIC TIP

Ideal for a sunny border where its richly scented flowers will give much pleasure and will also attract bees, butterflies and other insects into your garden.

HYDRANGEA

summer	hardy	semi-shade	18m/60ft	6m/20ft

The popular hybrids of the shrub *Hydrangea macrophylla* (1.8 × 1.8m/6 × 6ft) are known as Hortensias, with mop-heads of florets up to 20cm/8in wide, or Lacecaps, with smaller, open heads. Flowers are blue or pink. White-flowered species include *H. paniculata* and the climber *H. petiolaris*.

GROWING Plant in autumn or spring in a sheltered position in loamy, moisture-retentive soil previously enriched with well-rotted organic matter. *H. macrophylla* hybrids need top dressings of peat and an annual application of aluminium sulphate for blue flowers, or ground limestone for pink. Each spring, mulch with well-rotted organic matter and cut out damaged shoots. Remove faded flowerheads.

PROPAGATION Climbers: Take 7.5cm/3in cuttings in early summer and insert in a peat/sand mixture in a cold frame. Pot up individually when rooted, stand outdoors and set out in autumn. Shrubs: Take 15cm/6in cuttings in late summer *(see page 16)*.

SPECIES *H. petiolaris (above)*, self-supporting climber, 25cm/10in corymbs of cream flowers, early summer; *H. paniculata* 'Grandiflora', shrub with arching stems, maximum height 4.5m/15ft, 45cm/18in panicles of white flowers, late summer; *H. arborescens* 'Grandiflora', hardy American shrub, compact at 1.2 × 1.2m/4 × 4ft, pure white flowers all summer.

■ CUT FLOWER TIP

The spectacular flower heads are very popular with flower arrangers, but the faded heads can also be cut after flowering and dried for winter displays.

DEUTZIA

| summer | hardy | sun/semi-shade | 2m/6ft6in | 2m/6ft6in |

Most of the deutzias in cultivation are hybrids from parents of Asiatic origin. These rewarding shrubs are easy to grow and bear masses of pale pink, cerise or white star-shaped blooms in mid summer.

GROWING Plant in any type of fertile soil from autumn to spring, in full sun or in dappled shade. Avoid exposed sites. Prune after flowering, cutting back old flowering stems at ground level.

PROPAGATION Take 7.5cm/3in semi-ripe cuttings in late summer and place in a peat/sand mixture in a cold frame. Transfer the rooted cuttings to a nursery bed the following spring, grow on and plant out in the autumn.

SPECIES *Deutzia monbeigii*, arching stems, sheds bark to reveal orange-brown tints, abundant clusters of white flowers; *D. × hybrida*, strong-growing, of upright habit, older stems shed bark. The named variety 'Mont Rose' (*above*) bears large open flowers of rich rose ageing to white. *D. × rosea*, neat at 90cm/3ft high, pale pink bell-shaped flowers.

POSSIBLE PROBLEMS Severe cold may check vigour.

MAGNOLIA

| spring | hardy | semi-shade | 3m/10ft | 3m/10ft |

For many people, a magnolia blooming in early spring is the most beautiful sight of the gardening year. The shrubs of this much-admired genus bear magnificent white or pink flowers which are often fragrant.

GROWING Plant in spring in well-drained lime-free soil into which plenty of peat has been incorporated. Magnolias need a site giving protection from cold winds. Support with stakes for the first 3 or 4 years. Top-dress annually in spring with peat or leaf-mould. No pruning is needed.

PROPAGATION Magnolias may be raised from seed (germination takes up to 18 months), by cuttings taken in summer or by layering (*see page 17*) in spring.

SPECIES *Magnolia grandiflora*, evergreen with large, round creamy-white fragrant flowers. Excellent against a wall, where it can reach 10m/33ft. In this situation inward-growing shoots should be removed in spring. *M. stellata* (*above*), the hardiest species with white, star-shaped, fragrant flowers; the variety 'Royal Star' bears larger, more showy blooms. *M. soulangeana*, maximum height 5m/15ft, cup-shaped white flowers tinged carmine at the base open before the leaves unfurl; *M. liliiflora*, 2.4m/8ft, cup-shaped purple flowers.

POSSIBLE PROBLEMS Frost damage leading to grey mould.

■ SPECIAL CARE TIP

This shrub needs a fertile soil, so prepare the ground before planting by digging in some bonemeal – fish, blood and bone - or other general fertilizer. After planting, mulch with well-rotted compost or manure, and thereafter mulch each spring, which will also help to protect new growth against frost.

■ SPECIAL CARE TIP

These shrubs are not so difficult to grow as you may think. However, it does need some care when planting, and in selecting a well-dug, sunny site. A moisture-retentive soil is essential, so dig in plenty of compost before planting, and lay more well-rotted compost around the roots. Mulch well after planting.

CEANOTHUS

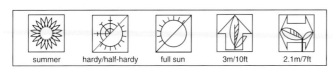

| summer | hardy/half-hardy | full sun | 3m/10ft | 2.1m/7ft |

This large genus of attractive evergreen and deciduous shrubs is often known as Californian lilac, revealing its origin. Most bear clusters of heavenly blue flowers; a few are pink or white.

GROWING Set out young plants in late spring in light, well-drained soil. Most types, especially the evergreen, need the protection of a warm, sunny wall, but will grow in the open if sheltered from wind. Tie shoots and branches of evergreens to wall supports and trim lightly when needed. Prune deciduous varieties in spring by cutting the preceding year's growth back to 7.5cm/3in. Remove faded flowerheads from all types.

PROPAGATION Take 7.5cm/3in soft cuttings in summer; root in sandy compost under cover; pot on when rooted and plant out the following year.

VARIETIES *Ceanothus* × 'Autumnal Blue', one of the hardier hybrids, evergreen, deep blue flowers; C. × 'Burkwoodii', evergreen, light blue, slightly scented flowers; C. × 'Gloire de Versailles', deciduous, panicles of powder blue flowers, a good choice for a sunny open site; C. *impressus* (above), half-hardy evergreen wall shrub, clusters of small deep blue flowers in spring; C. *thyrsiflorens repens*, evergreen, forms mounds 90cm/3ft high, light blue flowers in late spring.

POSSIBLE PROBLEMS Soils high in lime may sometimes cause chlorosis.

▤ PLANTING TIP

This shrub can be hard hit by severe winters, and especially by a hard frost. Ideally, position in a sheltered spot, or against a hot, dry wall in the sun.

IPOMOEA

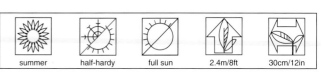

| summer | half-hardy | full sun | 2.4m/8ft | 30cm/12in |

Ipomoea tricolor is popularly known as morning glory, because its flowers open in the morning sunshine but fade by the end of the afternoon. A perennial grown as an annual, this climbing plant needs the support of netting or twiggy sticks for its twining stems. The funnel-shaped blooms are blue and white, up to 12.5cm/5in across.

GROWING Set out young plants in late spring or early summer after all danger of frost is past. Light but fertile soil is best, in a position sheltered from wind. Dead-head regularly and discard the plants after flowering is over.

PROPAGATION Sow seeds in spring under protection at 15°C/60°F, placing two seeds to a 9cm/3½in pot. Soak the seeds for 24 hours before planting to assist germination. Harden off the seedlings before transferring them to the permanent site. Alternatively, sow seeds where they are to grow in early summer.

VARIETIES 'Heavenly Blue' *(above)*: large flowers of clear sky blue; 'Sapphire Cross', purple-blue; 'Flying Saucers', very large flowers, blue and white striped.

POSSIBLE PROBLEMS Aphids on young shoots; night frost distorts young leaves.

▤ PLANTING TIP

Climbers such as morning glory can be used to hide unsightly items, such as an ugly chain-link fence. They can also be used to frame a window: grown in a container, this climber could be trained up lines of twine. It could also be trained up a narrow trellis on a patio to provide high-level interest.

Mahonia

| winter | hardy | sun/semi-shade | 3m/10ft | 2.4m/8ft |

Mahonias are handsome shrubs, with dark green glossy leaves and racemes of fragrant, bright yellow flowers. The foliage is often used as winter decoration. All the species bear dark blue berries; those of *Mahonia aquifolium* are carried in clusters, earning it the common name Oregon grape. This species spreads by means of suckers and is an excellent ground cover plant.

GROWING Set out young plants in autumn or spring in sun or semi-shade in fertile, well-drained soil that is not markedly alkaline. Mulch annually in spring with leaf-mould or peat. No pruning is necessary except for *M. aquifolium* grown as ground cover, which should be pruned hard each spring.

SPECIES *M. aquifolium*, maximum height 1.5m/5ft unless regularly pruned, spread 1.8m/6ft, spring-flowering, dense clusters of flowers precede plump berries, wind-tolerant. Leaves of the variety 'Atropurpurea' turn red in winter; *M. ×* 'Charity' *(above)*, hybrid, bearing 30cm/12in racemes of deep yellow flowers in mid winter.

POSSIBLE PROBLEMS Leaf spot; rust.

▌ PLANTING TIP

Good to plant as an informal hedge or as ground cover, especially in shaded conditions. For a small garden remember that the leaves are rather prickly.

Passiflora

| summer | half-hardy | full sun | 9m/30ft | 6m/20ft |

Passiflora umbellicata and *P. caerulea*, the common passion flower, are the only members of their family – natives of Brazil – that can be grown outdoors and even then they must have a sheltered site. They bear exotic, star-shaped flowers with prominent stamens, which are occasionally followed by golden egg-shaped fruits.

GROWING Plant in late spring in well-drained soil, in a sheltered position against a warm, sunny wall with trelliswork or wire mesh for support. Tie in the young growths until the tendrils take over. Protect with cloches over winter. Plants may be cut down by frost but new shoots arise from the base. Prune in spring if necessary, removing overcrowded or frost-damaged stems.

PROPAGATION Take 7.5cm/3in stem cuttings in summer and place in a peat/sand mixture in a propagator at 16°C/61°F until rooted. Pot up individually and grow on. Harden off before planting out the following spring.

SPECIES *P. caerulea (above)*, vigorous plant with dense habit, white-petalled flowers 7.5cm/3in across have purple stamens. The variety 'Constance Elliot' is all white and hardier than the species; *P. umbellicata*, maximum height 6m/20ft, large purplish flowers.

POSSIBLE PROBLEMS Cucumber mosaic virus discolours the leaves.

▌ PLANTING TIP

This beautiful climber will enhance any wall or fence when grown up trellis or netting for support. On a patio, it can easily be grown in a pot or other container against a wall, and this climber actually flowers better when it has some root restriction.

CLEMATIS HYBRIDS

| summer | hardy | full sun | 1.8-2.4m/6-8ft | 1.2-1.8m/4-6ft |

Clematis are universally popular climbers, scrambling over a wall or fence, trellis or arbour, and covered with open star-shaped flowers of white, blue, pink or purple. There is a huge choice of beautiful hybrids. Some flower twice, in early and mid summer; others bloom from mid summer onwards.

GROWING Plant deeply between autumn and spring, preferably in alkaline soil, in a position where the base will be shaded from strong sun. Support for the twining stalks is essential. Prune those that flower twice by cutting back the shoots to 23cm/9in the second spring after planting. Remove all weak growth each spring and tie in replacement shoots. For summer-flowering clematis, train the shoots across wires at 30cm/12in from the ground and the flowering stems will grow upwards. Cut back flowered stems each spring to two good buds. Mulch each spring.

PROPAGATION Layer 18-month-old shoots in spring (see page 18).

VARIETIES Early-flowering: 'Belle of Woking', double, silvery-mauve; 'Maureen', velvety purple; 'Lincoln Star', rich pink; 'Nellie Moser' (above), pale mauve, crimson stripe. Summer-flowering: 'Huldine', pearly white; 'Etoile Violette', deep purple with cream stamens; 'Gravetye Beauty', cherry red.

POSSIBLE PROBLEMS Clematis wilt; powdery mildew.

▥ PLANTING TIP

To keep the roots moist and shaded after planting, cover the soil with flat stones and plant low shrubs and creepers to shield the base from the sun.

CLEMATIS SPECIES

| spring | hardy | full sun | 9m/30ft | 15m/50ft |

Species clematis bear smaller flowers than the showy hybrids, but they are beautiful climbing plants that merit a place in any garden.

GROWING Treat as hybrids. Shade for the root-run can be provided by low shrubs. To prune, remove only weak growths and shorten the remainder by two thirds.

PROPAGATION Species can be raised from seed sown in autumn in pans of compost in a cold frame. After germination, in the following spring, pot up singly and set outdoors, transferring to the permanent site in autumn.

SPECIES *Clematis armandii*, vigorous evergreen, glossy foliage, white saucer-shaped flowers 6cm/2½in across; *C. orientalis*, fern-like leaves, abundant nodding scented yellow flowers in late summer followed by large silver seedheads; *C. tangutica*, grey-green leaves, lantern-shaped yellow flowers in late summer, attractive seed-heads; *C. flammula*, height 3m/10ft, bears a mass of tangled growth at the top with 30cm/12in panicles of fragrant white flowers in late summer/early autumn; *C. montana* (above), 12 × 6m/40 × 20ft, easiest species to cultivate, profuse white flowers; the pink-flowered variety 'Rubens' is very popular.

POSSIBLE PROBLEMS Clematis wilt; powdery mildew.

▥ PLANTING TIP

Clematis are rapid climbers that will quickly cover a wall, pergola, fence or even an unsightly building. They can also be used to scramble over an existing bush or tree, such as a dead apple tree. If you allow them to scramble through a flowering bush or tree, take colour into account to avoid clashes.

R HODODENDRON

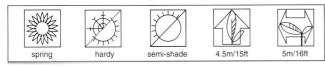

| spring | hardy | semi-shade | 4.5m/15ft | 5m/16ft |

Rhododendrons have much to offer gardeners who must work with acid soil. The magnificent flowers come in an unparalleled range of colours. In size the plants range from as low as 30cm/12in to an imposing 4.5m/15ft or more and spread wide. About 800 species are known and thousands of hybrids have been developed.

GROWING Plant in early autumn in well-drained but moisture-retentive acid soil. Most prefer light shade but hardy hybrids and small-leaved types tolerate full sun. Water well and mulch after planting. Remove dead flowerheads. Prune to restrict growth if necessary by cutting back lightly to a whorl of leaves in spring. Old, straggly hardy hybrids can be induced to make new compact growth if pruned heavily in late winter.

PROPAGATION Increase stock by layering *(see page 17)* or cuttings *(see Azalea)*. Varieties do not come true from seed.

VARIETIES 'Bluebird', 90cm/3ft high, rich violet flowers; 'Praecox', 1.5m/5ft, rose-purple, very early flowering; 'Scarlet Wonder', 60cm/24in, compact shape. Hardy hybrids (all these up to 4.5m/15 ft, late spring-flowering): 'Cynthia', rose-crimson, vigorous grower; 'Mount Everest', white with red throat, fragrant; 'Purple Splendour', purple marked black.

POSSIBLE PROBLEMS Rhododendron leafhopper causes bud-blast disease; rhododendron bugs suck sap from the leaves.

■ ORGANIC TIP

If your soil is too alkaline, grow rhododendrons by constructing a raised bed with a wooden framework, or peat block walls, filled with a peaty mixture.

A ZALEA

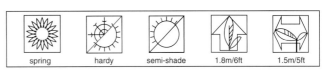

| spring | hardy | semi-shade | 1.8m/6ft | 1.5m/5ft |

Azaleas are types of rhododendrons, but generally smaller; the deciduous azaleas do not have scaly leaves, and the so-called evergreens actually drop some leaves in autumn. The showy flowers are bell-, funnel- or saucer-shaped.

GROWING *See Rhododendron.*

PROPAGATION Deciduous azaleas may be increased by layering *(see page 17)*, rhododendrons (hardy hybrids), Kurume and other evergreen azaleas from cuttings. Take cuttings from young growths in summer and place in a mixture of sand and sifted peat at 2:1 in a cold frame. When firmly rooted pot up in a compost consisting of equal parts (by volume) of sifted peat, leaf-mould, lime-free loam and sand. Keep lightly moist, protect over winter and plant out in nursery beds in spring. The compact root system makes transplanting easy. In fact, if a plant outgrows its site, it is sometimes better to move it than prune it.

SPECIES Evergreens (give shelter from cold winds): 'Palestrina' *(above)*, pure white; 'Orange Beauty', soft orange; 'Fedora', deep pink. Kurume hybrids (small glossy leaves, slightly tender): 'Kirin', rose-pink; 'Hinodegiri', carmine-red. Ghent azaleas (deciduous, hardy, fragrant): 'Corneille', double flowers, cream flushed pink; 'Narcissiflora', primrose yellow.

POSSIBLE PROBLEMS *See Rhododendron*; azalea whitefly infest the undersides of the leaves.

■ SPECIAL CARE TIP

Azaleas, are like rhododendrons and thrive on acid, peaty soil. They also enjoy dappled shade and need shelter from frosts, which can blacken their blooms. If your soil has a trace of lime, water the foliage with sequestered-iron solution and mulch generously with peat.

FUCHSIA

summer	hardy	full sun	90cm/3ft	90cm/3ft

So-called greenhouse fuchsias will not survive the winter out-doors. Fortunately there are a number of hardy fuchsias with the beautiful characteristic bell-like flowers which make decorative bushes or hedges. In cold districts they may die back above ground in winter, but shoot up afresh the next spring.

GROWING Plant in early summer when there is no longer any danger of night frost, in well-drained soil previously enriched with peat or leaf-mould. A sheltered spot is best. Water well in dry weather. In cold districts, cut the plants back to ground level in the autumn and sprinkle a shovelful of coarse grit around the crown before the first frosts. In warmer areas, simply cut out damaged wood in spring.

PROPAGATION Take 10cm/4in tip cuttings without flower buds in spring. Insert in individual pots of a peat/sand mixture at 16°C/61°F. Pot on when rooted and pinch out both leading and lateral shoots frequently to encourage bushy growth. Overwinter at 13°C/55°F and plant out in early summer.

SPECIES *Fuchsia magellanica*, hardiest species, about 1.5m/5ft, more as hedging in mild areas; crimson and purple flowers. Varieties include 'Gracilis', slender leaves and flowers; 'Gracilis Versicolor', beautifully variegated leaves; 'Pumila', only 15cm/6in; 'Alba', pale pink flowers; 'Mrs Popple' *(above)* profusion of large flowers.

POSSIBLE PROBLEMS Generally trouble-free.

■ SPECIAL CARE TIP

Hardy garden fuchsias will survive the winter, though they may die back completely. Mulch crowns heavily with compost when growth dies down, to protect from cold and frost. In the spring, prune back the previous year's growth to ground level. Clip fuchsia hedges in the spring.

CAMELLIA

winter/spring	hardy	semi-shade	5m/16ft	3.6m/12ft

Camellias are beautiful, with large cup-shaped flowers of pink, red, purple or white and dark green glossy leaves.

GROWING Plant in autumn or spring in any good, lime-free soil, previously enriched with leaf-mould if light in texture. Give plants the protection of a sheltered wall which is shaded from the rising sun, since they are susceptible to damage from wind, frost and early morning sun after frost. Stake young plants until established. Mulch generously every spring with well-rotted organic matter or leaf-mould. Dead-head the species after flowering. If necessary, shorten wispy shoots in spring – no other pruning is required. Early-flowering species do well in small tubs containing a mixture of lime-free loam, peat and sand at 4:2:1, but should be moved indoors over winter.

PROPAGATION Layer specimens in autumn *(see page 17)*.

SPECIES *Camellia japonica (above)*, very early flowering, all shades of pink. Varieties include 'White Swan', single white flowers with prominent yellow stamens; 'Adolphe Audusson', semi-double crimson flowers 12.5cm/5in across; 'Anemonae-flora', deep red flowers; 'Elegans', large rose-pink peony-type flowers. *C. × williamsii*, outstanding hybrid, height up to 2.4m/8ft, free-flowering from late autumn to spring. Varieties include the exceptional 'Donation', pale pink.

POSSIBLE PROBLEMS Birds may damage the flowers.

■ ORGANIC TIP

If your soil is slightly chalky, you can grow this shrub by giving an annual dose of sequestered iron, seaweed fertilizer in the spring and a peat

SPIRAEA

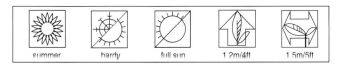

| summer | hardy | full sun | 1.2m/4ft | 1.5m/5ft |

Spiraeas bear tiny star-shaped flowers of white or shades of pink in flat or plume-shaped clusters. They are good subjects for a mixed border and are often grown as decorative hedging.

GROWING Plant between autumn and spring in deep, rich soil in an open sunny position. Prune *Spiraea × bumalda* and *S. japonica* in early spring, cutting back to 10cm/4in from ground level. Remove dead flowerheads. Thin out all species after flowering. Young plants for hedging should be set between 38 and 60cm/15 and 24in apart. Cut back the previous season's growth to within 15cm/6in of ground level after planting. Trim established hedges every year.

PROPAGATION Lift, divide and replant between autumn and spring. Or, take 10cm/4in cuttings of half-ripe side shoots in summer and insert in sandy soil in a cold frame. Transfer to a nursery bed the next spring and plant out in the autumn.

SPECIES *S. × arguta*, commonly known as bridal wreath, a beautiful hybrid bearing umbels of pure white flowers on arching stems in spring, max height 2.4m/8ft, excellent underplanted with crocuses or cyclamen; *S. × bumalda*, hybrid bearing 12.5cm/5in wide heads of bright pink flowers; 'Anthony Waterer' (*above*) is a popular variety with foliage variegated cream and pink when young; *S. × japonica*, maximum height 1.5m/5ft, large pink flowerheads on erect stems.

POSSIBLE PROBLEMS Leaves may be stripped by sawfly.

■ ORGANIC TIP

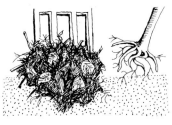

Spiraeas like sandy or alkaline soils, but these may need enriching before planting. Dig in well-rotted compost to help retain moisture and nutrients.

ENKIANTHUS

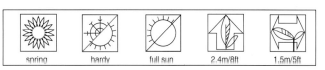

| spring | hardy | full sun | 2.4m/8ft | 1.5m/5ft |

Enkianthus campanulatus is a native of Japan and is prized for its foliage – dull green in spring and summer, vivid scarlet in autumn. Its abundant bell-shaped flowers are creamy-yellow, tipped and veined rose-pink. There are no named varieties.

GROWING Plant in autumn or spring in acid or neutral soil. Peat or leaf-mould should be added to ordinary lime-free soils. A sunny sheltered position, as in light woodland, is preferred. Pruning is generally unnecessary, but leggy overgrown species may be cut back hard in late winter.

PROPAGATION Take 7.5cm/3in heeled cuttings of lateral shoots in late summer and insert in a peat and sand mixture in a cold frame. Transfer the rooted cuttings to a nursery bed in spring to grow on for 2-3 years before planting them out in their permanent positions.

POSSIBLE PROBLEMS Generally trouble-free.

■ PLANTING TIP

Otherwise known as the pagoda bush, because of its vivid colouring. If your garden is successful with rhododendrons and azaleas, you will succeed with this shrub. Lime-free soil is essential; dig peat into the soil when planting, and mulch with peat.

SHRUBS

FLORIBUNDA ROSES

| summer | hardy | full sun | 90cm/3ft | 60cm/24in |

Floribunda roses are derived from the early hybrid teas, and have similar foliage. Whether matt or glossy, there are 7 oval leaflets, sometimes flushed red when young. These roses are very thorny. Flowering twice, in mid summer and early autumn, they bear their 7.5cm/3in wide blooms in large terminal clusters, and are good for borders and decorative hedges.

GROWING If conditions are favourable, roses may be planted at any time from late autumn to spring. Rich, loamy soil gives the best results. Prepare the site by digging it over well and mixing in plenty of well-rotted organic matter. Double-digging is recommended. Make a hole big enough to spread out the roots. Mix a bucketful of peat with a cupful of sterilized bonemeal and place 3 cupfuls of this mixture in each planting hole. Make sure the union of the rootstock and the rose is just below ground level. Give a mulch of partially rotted manure or well-rotted compost every other spring, and a mulch of leaves (rotted or unrotted) each autumn to conserve moisture. For pruning *see Hybrid Tea Roses.*

PROPAGATION Increase by budding (*see page 18*).

VARIETIES 'Iceberg' (*above*), 1.5m/5ft, large sprays of white, fragrant blooms, good for hedging; 'City of Birmingham', abundant scarlet blooms with wavy petals; 'Korresia', sweetly fragrant, golden yellow.

POSSIBLE PROBLEMS *See Hybrid Tea Roses.*

▧ DRIED FLOWER TIP

Roses are lovely as cut flowers, but they can also be dried. The best roses for drying should have long, stiff stems and flowers that are well-formed but not so dense as to make drying difficult. Roses can be dried by hanging in the dark, in warm air, but it is best to use silica gel and follow manufacturer's instructions.

OLD ROSES

| summer | hardy | full sun | 1.5m/5ft | 1.5m/5ft |

Descended from true *Rosa* species such as *R. alba* (the White Rose of York) and *R. damascena* (damask rose), old roses were popular before hybrid teas were introduced, and are now enjoying a well-deserved revival. Intensely fragrant, the blooms of white, pink or red have a relatively brief flowering period.

GROWING *See Floribunda Roses.* Albas, Damasks and Gallicas do not need rich soil. Prune the spring after planting by removing weak and damaged wood. For established bushes just remove straggly stems and any laterals that bore flowers the previous year. Do not prune until flowering is over.

PROPAGATION Take cuttings in late summer (*see page 16*).

VARIETIES Moss Roses (from *R. centifolia*), stems and branches covered with bristles. Very fragrant flowers 7.5cm/3in across: 'Henri Martin' (*above*), semi-double, deep pink; 'Comtesse de Murinais', vigorous shrub, pure white flowers with green centre. Gallicas (from *R. gallica*, the French rose), stiff stems, double flowers 5-7.5cm/2-3in wide: 'Cardinal Richelieu', pale pink ageing to deep purple, good for hedging. Bourbon roses (from *R. × odorata* and *R. damascena*) Globular or cup-shaped flowers in bloom from early summer to first frost: 'Boule de Neige', white; 'La Reine Victoria', deep pink.

POSSIBLE PROBLEMS *See Hybrid Tea Roses.*

▧ ORGANIC TIP

Roses appreciate a rich, well-fed soil, and well-rotted compost is the best medium for your old roses. If you provide a well-dug soil, enriched with well-rotted compost and manure before planting, and then mulch regularly with more, your roses will have no need of artificial fertilizer or rose feeds.

HYBRID TEA ROSES

summer	hardy	full sun	1.2m/4ft	60cm/24in

Hybrid tea roses were first raised in the late nineteenth century and are distinguished by a high pointed centre surrounded by petals that curve back. Excellent for cutting, the colour range is extensive, and some varieties are scented.

GROWING *See Floribunda Roses*. This group is particularly susceptible to damage by wind and rain. Prune autumn-planted roses hard in the first spring to encourage strong shoots from the base. Remove all damaged wood then cut back to 3 buds (4 or 5 for floribundas). Spring-planted roses can be pruned immediately. Once established, remove dead and damaged wood early each spring and cut back all the previous season's growth by two-thirds (by one-third for floribundas)

PROPAGATION By budding only (*see page 18*).

VARIETIES 'Bonsoir' (*above*) or the following which are all fragrant: 'Alec's Red', deep red; 'Ingrid Bergman', dark red; 'Royal William', crimson velvet; 'Iced Ginger'; 'Just Joey', coppery-orange; 'Tynwald', cream; 'Pink Pearl'; 'Prima Ballerina', deep rose-pink; 'Lover's Meeting', soft tangerine; 'Fragrant Cloud', coral-scarlet; 'Peer Gynt', yellow shaded peach; 'St Hugh's', creamy-yellow; 'Valencia', orange-bronze (prize-winning scent).

POSSIBLE PROBLEMS Aphids; caterpillars; sawfly larvae. Black spot; die-back; grey mould; rust; powdery mildew.

▇ ORGANIC TIP

Help to avoid aphid attacks in your rose garden by using the companion planting method. Plant tagetes, calendula or nasturtiums nearby to attract hoverflies.

CLIMBING ROSES

summer	hardy	full sun	6m/20ft	4.5m/15ft

All gardens, whatever their style, are enhanced by a climbing rose – or two. Climbers with species roses as parents are very vigorous (up to 9m/30ft), bearing 5cm/2in wide cream or yellow flowers in mid summer; climbers bred from hybrid teas are a better choice for more restricted areas such as pillars or fences, and bear flowers up to 12.5cm/5in wide.

GROWING *See Floribunda Roses*. Always plant climbing roses close to their supports. To prune, cut back strong growths after planting to 38cm/15in, weaker ones to within 10cm/4in of the base. Thereafter prune in early spring, leaving the basic framework but cutting back short laterals to 2-3 buds. Tie in new shoots in autumn.

VARIETIES The following are suitable for restricted areas: 'Caroline Testout', profusion of heavily fragrant, double pink flowers; 'Meg', pink and apricot; 'Danse du Feu', double, orange-scarlet; 'Golden Showers', pale gold; 'Parkdirektor Riggers', scarlet; 'Zephirine Drouhin', a bourbon rose, bright pink, fragrant, continuous flowering. Strong growers: 'Mme Gregoire Staechelin', clear pink, fragrant; 'Wedding Day', very vigorous, yellow in bud opening white; 'Mermaid', large, butter-yellow, fragrant, good on a cold wall. 'Fantin Latour' (*above*) double flowers over a short summer period.

POSSIBLE PROBLEMS *See Hybrid Tea Roses*. Climbers are particularly susceptible to powdery mildew.

▇ ORGANIC TIP

Powdery mildew is at its worst when the plant roots are dry. Avoid by mulching well in the spring with well-rotted manure or compost and renew if necessary.

SYRINGA

spring	hardy	sun/semi-shade	3.6m/12ft	3m/10ft

Syringa vulgaris, the common lilac, is one of the best-loved garden shrubs. There are a number of varieties, some double-flowered, all of them fragrant. Lilacs are deciduous, bearing panicles of white, lilac, pink or purple flowers up to 25cm/10in long in late spring.

GROWING Plant in autumn in sun or semi-shade on any type of fertile soil. Lilacs take 1-2 years to become established. Remove all the flowers in the first season to reserve the plant's energies. In later years dead-head after flowering. Remove lower buds and branches to form a single stem if desired. Pull off any suckers that appear. Prune old, straggly bushes in late autumn, cutting back to 90cm/3ft from ground level.

PROPAGATION Take 10cm/4in half-ripe cuttings with a heel in summer and insert in a peat/sand mixture in a propagator at 16°C/61°F. Pot up when rooted and grow on in a cold frame. Transfer to a nursery bed in the spring and grow on for 2 years before planting out.

VARIETIES 'Candeur', cream; 'Firmament', pale blue; 'Massena', deep purple; 'Maud Notcutt', the best white; 'Mrs Edward Harding', double, red; 'Marechal Foch', cerise; 'Primrose', pale yellow; 'Paul Thirion', double, rose-red, very fragrant; 'Souvenir de Louis Spaeth' *(above)*.

POSSIBLE PROBLEMS Frost damage leading to grey mould; lilac blight.

▦ ORGANIC TIP

The sweet-smelling flowers attract butterflies and other nectar-loving insects into the garden in early summer, when food may be in short supply.

ERICA

winter	hardy	full sun	25cm/10in	60cm/24in

The winter-flowering heath, *Erica carnea* syn. *E. herbacea*, is a low-growing shrub excellent for ground cover and, unlike other heaths, will tolerate chalky soils. The foliage is usually green, sometimes golden, the bell-shaped flowers white or pink. Easy to grow, heaths are invaluable in low-maintenance gardens and wherever winter colour is needed.

GROWING An open sunny position is essential. Prepare the site by digging it over well. Mix bonemeal into the top soil at 100g/m² (4oz/sq yd) and top dress with a 7.5cm/3in layer of peat. Plant in spring or late autumn, making sure the plants are well firmed in with the stem completely buried. Set the plants between 30 and 45cm/12 and 18in apart in groups of 6 or more. Water well – do not let plants dry out, particularly in the first year. Cut right back after flowering to keep the plants dense and bushy.

PROPAGATION Take 5cm/2in cuttings of side shoots in late summer and insert in pots of a moist mixture of sharp sand and peat at 2:1. Place in a mist propagator until rooted and transfer to a cold frame or nursery bed. Plant out when 10cm/4in high.

VARIETIES 'Cecilia M. Beale', white, and 'Eileen Porter', pink *(together above)*; 'Aurea', golden leaves, pink blooms; 'Praecox Rubra', prostrate with pink flowers.

POSSIBLE PROBLEMS Generally trouble-free.

▦ DRIED FLOWER TIP

All ericas are very easy to dry, including native wild heather, and preserve their vivid colouring. Simply hang up bunches in a draughty, warm place and allow to dry naturally. It is best to cut bunches or erica before the flowers are fully out.

L AVANDULA

| summer | hardy | full sun | 1.2m/4ft | 1.2m/4ft |

H IBISCUS

| summer/autumn | hardy | full sun | 3m/10ft | 1.8m/6ft |

Lavandula spica, the common lavender, richly deserves its popularity. Evergreen and intensely fragrant, it makes a charming low-growing hedge or edging to a pathway. The flowers may be dried and are often used in pot-pourri mixtures. Herbalists use a lavender infusion on a cold compress to treat headaches.

GROWING Plant between autumn and spring in any type of well-drained soil. Remove flowerheads when faded. Trim the plants with shears in late summer, and cut right back in spring to encourage bushy growth. For hedges, set young plants 23-30cm/9-12in apart. Trim established hedges in spring.

PROPAGATION Take 10cm/4in cuttings of non-flowering shoots in late summer and insert in a peat/sand mixture in a cold frame. Overwinter in the frame and plant out in the spring. Alternatively take 20cm/8in cuttings in early autumn and insert them where they are to grow.

VARIETIES 'Hidcote' syn. 'Nana Atropurpurea' *(above)*: compact at maximum height 60cm/24in, deep blue flowers; 'Alba': white; 'Twickle Purple': up to 90cm/3ft high, flower-spikes up to 12.5 cm/5in long.

POSSIBLE PROBLEMS Frost damage leading to grey mould; honey fungus.

The hibiscus belongs to the mallow family, and bears the beautiful characteristic funnel-shaped flowers in late summer and into the autumn. The blooms may be pink, white, blue or red and measure up to 7.5cm/3in across. Only one species, *H. syriacus*, is hardy enough for outdoor cultivation. This attractive shrub is suitable for the back of a mixed border.

GROWING Plant between autumn and spring in any type of well-drained soil in full sun. In cold districts it is necessary to give plants the protection of a wall. No regular pruning is necessary, but straggly shoots may be shortened after flowering.

PROPAGATION Take 10cm/4in cuttings of non-flowering lateral shoots in summer and insert in a peat/sand mixture at 16°C/61°F. When rooted, pot up individually and place in a cold frame over winter. Pot on in late spring, set outdoors and transfer to the flowering site in the autumn.

VARIETIES 'Blue Bird', blue with red centre; 'Coeleste', deep blue; 'Hamabo', white flowers flushed pink, crimson centres; 'Woodbridge' *(above)*, rosy pink, red centre. Double-flowered varieties include 'Violaceus Plenus', wine-red; 'Elegantissimus', white, red centre; 'Ardens', mauve-tinted rose.

POSSIBLE PROBLEMS Aphids; buds drop if soil dries out.

▓ DRIED FLOWER TIP

Lavender dries to a lovely faded blue. To dry, pick when in full flower on a dry sunny day (never after rain or dew). Hang upside down in a dry place.

▓ SPECIAL CARE TIP

This shrub is not for every garden - it needs full sun, a well-drained soil, and protection from cold winds, eg against a wall. If these conditions are not possible, grow in container or tub on a sheltered terrace or in a conservatory or greenhouse.

WISTARIA

| spring | hardy | full sun | 30m/100ft | 18m/60ft |

Wistaria sinensis, or Chinese wistaria, is one of the loveliest climbing shrubs – and potentially one of the largest, though annual pruning will keep it within more reasonable bounds. Its twining habit can be supported by an arch or an old tree; against a wall, permanent supports are essential. The leaves consist of numerous delicate leaflets; before they are developed glorious lilac-blue or white flowers appear, in racemes up to 30cm/12in long.

GROWING Plant in autumn or spring on any good soil. The site should afford adequate room for root growth. A warm, sunny wall is ideal. Tie the young growths in to the supports. Pruning is advisable to encourage flowering; left alone, plants take up to 10 years to come into flower. Prune in winter, cutting back all growths to within 2-3 buds of the base of the previous year's growth. In summer, train the long leaders in the desired direction.

PROPAGATION By layering (*see page 17*).

VARIETIES The species with lilac-blue flowers is reliable and popular. 'Alba' (*above*) bears a mass of white flowers; 'Plena' has double mauve flowers.

POSSIBLE PROBLEMS Birds may damage buds and flowers; aphids; thrips. Bud-drop if soil dries out or night temperatures are very cold.

CHOISYA

| spring | hardy | full sun | 2m/6 ft 6in | 2m/6 ft 6in |

The Mexican orange blossom, *Choisya ternata*, is one of the most accommodating of evergreens. An attractively rounded shrub, its three-part leaves are a dark glossy green and give off a pungent aromatic scent when crushed. A multitude of white, sweet-scented flowers appear in late spring. There are no named varieties.

GROWING Plant in spring in any type of well-drained soil. Full sun is best but semi-shade is tolerated. In cold districts it is best to site plants against a warm, sunny wall. No regular pruning is required, but any frost-damaged leaves or shoots should be cut out in early spring. As soon as flowering is over, cut out any straggly shoots.

PROPAGATION Take 7.5cm/3in cuttings of half-ripe lateral shoots in late summer and place in a peat/sand mixture at 16°C/61°F. When rooted, pot up the cuttings singly and over-winter in a cold frame. Pot on in the spring, set outdoors and plant out the following spring. In cold areas, transfer the pots to a cold frame over winter.

POSSIBLE PROBLEMS Frost damage; honey fungus.

■ PLANTING TIP

The most vigorous variety is W. sinensis, but if grown against a wall, special attention is needed, as it can destroy guttering and get under the roof tiles.

If grown against a house wall, it is safer to grow the less vigorous Floribunda or macroborys - the latter has flowers 75cm/2 ½ feet long.

■ PLANTING TIP

This is one of the neatest garden shrubs, forming a dome of glossy leaves, making it particularly suitable for a small town garden or patio.

LONICERA

summer	hardy	semi-shade	6m/20ft	3.6m/12ft

The deciduous climber *Lonicera periclymenum*, better known as woodbine or honeysuckle, is a familiar sight in the wild, twining its stems in strong bands around anything in reach. The cultivated varieties will do the same in the garden, given wires, trellis or an old tree to scramble over. The beautiful tubular flowers have a delicious fragrance.

GROWING Plant from autumn to spring in any type of well-drained soil, previously enriched with humus. Honeysuckles like their roots in shade and the tops in sun. Give a light mulch of leaf-mould or well-rotted compost each spring. Prune after flowering if necessary to remove old wood.

PROPAGATION Take 10cm/4in stem cuttings in summer and place in a peat/sand mixture in a cold frame. When rooted, pot up individually and set outside. Transfer to the flowering site in the late autumn.

VARIETIES 'Serotina' (late Dutch honeysuckle), bushy habit, flowers red outside, cream within; 'Belgica' (early Dutch honeysuckle), red and yellow flowers appear in late spring. These two varieties planted together will provide flowers for a six-month period.

POSSIBLE PROBLEMS Leaf spot; powdery mildew.

VIBURNUM

winter	hardy	full sun	2.4m/8ft	1.8m/6ft

There are some 200 species of viburnum, most of them hardy, some evergreen. One of the best evergreens is *V. tinus* or laurustinus, which bears its flat heads of white flowers from late autumn through to the end of spring.

GROWING Plant in the autumn or spring on fertile, moisture-retentive soil, in a position sheltered from cold winds. Do not site the plants where early morning sun after frosts could damage young growths. Prune in late spring, simply removing old and damaged branches.

PROPAGATION Take 7.5cm/3in cuttings of lateral shoots with a heel in early summer. Place in a peat/sand mixture in a propagator at 16°C/61°F. Pot up individually when rooted and set in a cold frame. Keep in the frame over winter. Transfer to nursery rows in the spring and grow on for 2-3 years before planting in the permanent site.

VARIETIES 'Variegatum': leaves splashed with gold; 'French White', pure white flowers; 'Eve Price', dense shrub with pink flowers.

POSSIBLE PROBLEMS White flies on underside of leaves; frost damage leading to grey mould.

ORGANIC TIP

An absolute must for the organic garden. Beautifully scented flowers attract bees and other insects into the garden. They also attract moths in the evening, when the scent is strongest. The red berries which follow flowering are enjoyed by the birds.

CUT FLOWER TIP

The wonderfully perfumed flowers of this shrub make it a delight in a border, and a few branches will scent a whole room in a winter arrangement.

PIERIS

| spring | hardy | semi-shade | 3.6m/12ft | 4.5m/15ft |

Pieris formosa is a shapely evergreen shrub, the leaves of which are a warm red when young and turn green later. It bears drooping panicles of lily-of-the-valley-like flowers in late spring. Pieris are handsome slow-growing shrubs which may be planted as specimens or in a mixed border.

GROWING Lime-free soil is essential. Set out young plants in autumn or spring in a sheltered position. Do not allow the soil to dry out during the summer. Give an annual top-dressing of leaf-mould or peat in spring. Pruning is minimal – simply remove faded flowerheads and cut back straggling shoots at the same time.

PROPAGATION Take 10cm/4in cuttings of half-ripe shoots in late summer and place in sandy soil in a cold frame. Pot up individually the following spring, using a mixture of equal parts of peat, loam, leaf-mould and sand. Keep in the cold frame, transferring to a nursery bed in the autumn to grow on for 2-3 years before planting in their permanent positions.

VARIETIES 'Forrestii' (*above*), noted for the vivid red of the young foliage and quantity of flowers.

POSSIBLE PROBLEMS Generally trouble-free.

▓ PLANTING TIP

An acid soil is essential for this plant. Dig in plenty of peat and compost before planting, and mulch with more peat after planting. In following years, mulch with peat every spring to top up the acidity.

CHAENOMELES

| spring | hardy | full sun | 90cm/3ft | 1.5m/5ft |

There are four species of chaenomeles in cultivation, collectively known as flowering quinces. They bear red, pink or white flowers like apple blossom, followed by small round yellow fruits. The plants, though attractive, have an untidy habit of growth and look best in an informal garden.

GROWING Plant from autumn to spring in any type of soil, even clay, in a sunny position or against a wall. In the open, the only pruning necessary is the thinning of overcrowded branches after flowering. If grown against a wall, cut back the previous season's growth to 2-3 buds after flowering.

PROPAGATION By layering (*see page 17*). Alternatively take 10cm/4in cuttings of lateral shoots with a heel in late summer. Insert in a peat/sand mixture in a propagator at 16°C/61°F. When rooted pot up the cuttings individually and overwinter in a cold frame. Plant out in the spring.

SPECIES *C. japonica* (Maule's quince, *above*), spreading shrub, coral-red flowers; named varieties include 'Brilliant', scarlet flowers. *C. speciosa* syn. *C. lagenaria* (Japanese quince), widely grown species, 1.8 × 1.8m/6 × 6ft in the open, higher on a wall, very early flowering. Named varieties include 'Apple Blossom', double pink flowers; 'Crown of Gold', deep red with showy yellow stamens; 'Fascination', orange; 'Nivalis', white.

POSSIBLE PROBLEMS Birds may damage flowers; chlorosis on very alkaline soils.

▓ PLANTING TIP

This early-flowering shrub is perfect for training against a fence or wall. It does well in partial shade, but is best in full sun. Trim back after flowering.

PYRACANTHA

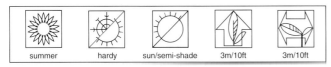

| summer | hardy | sun/semi-shade | 3m/10ft | 3m/10ft |

Firethorns are evergreen shrubs chiefly grown for their bright berries which stay from early autumn, after the flowers have faded, right through the winter. They look splendid against a wall, but as clipped hedges the berries will be relatively few.

GROWING Plant container-grown plants between autumn and spring in any fertile, well-drained soil. Wall-grown plants need trelliswork or a system of horizontal wires for support. During the summer tie in strong growths and trim the plant lightly. Plants for hedging should be set about 45cm/18in apart. Pinch out the growing points of young shoots when they are 20cm/8in long. Established hedges should be cut to shape in summer. Plants grown as bushes need no pruning.

PROPAGATION Take 10cm/4in cuttings of young shoots in summer and place in a peat/sand mixture in a propagator at 16°C/61°F. When rooted, pot up individually and transfer to a cold frame over winter. Pot on in the spring and set the pots outdoors in a bed of soil or peat. Plant out in the autumn.

VARIETIES *Pyracantha atalantioides* 'Aurea' (*above*), fast-growing, deep green leaves of variable shape, white flowers precede bright yellow berries; *P. crenulata* 'Rogersiana', abundant white flowers, orange-red berries; *P. × watereri* is a compact hybrid between these two producing masses of scarlet berries.

POSSIBLE PROBLEMS Woolly aphids; fireblight

ORGANIC TIP

This colourful shrub is ideal for attracting birds into your garden. The berries will provide food during the hard winter months when food is scarce.

FOTHERGILLA

| spring | hardy | full sun | 2.4m/8ft | 1.8m/6ft |

Native to the United States, fothergillas are handsome shrubs highly valued for the brilliant tints of their autumn foliage. The flowers are composed not of petals but numerous white stamens arranged in bottle-brush-like spikes. Sweetly scented, they appear in spring before the leaves unfurl.

GROWING Plant in late autumn or spring in light, lime-free soil into which peat or humus has previously been incorporated. Fothergillas tolerate light shade. No pruning is necessary.

PROPAGATION By layering in autumn (*see page 17*). The layers generally take 2 years to take root, at which point they may be separated from the parent plant and transferred to their permanent sites.

SPECIES *Fothergilla major*, oval mid-green leaves, grey-blue underneath, take on orange, yellow or red colouring in autumn; *F. monticola*, leaves completely green when young, red or orange in autumn, of more spreading habit than *F. major*.

POSSIBLE PROBLEMS Generally trouble-free.

PROPAGATION TIP

This is another plant that must have a peaty, lime-free soil. When layering, it is essential to bury the stem in a hole filled with peat, for it to take root success-fully. It will take 6-12 months to form roots. The rooted plantlet should then be planted out, again in a peaty soil.

TREES

Planting a tree is a sign of faith in the future. Most are planted at 3-4 years old and take about 30 years to reach their ultimate size (the sizes given in the entries in this chapter).

When you take over an established garden the chances are that you will inherit some trees, which, if you are lucky, will be mature, beautiful and in the right place. But even if they are not, cutting down a tree is a drastic measure from which many gardeners recoil. To be realistic, a garden cannot succeed if it is dominated by huge trees that literally put everything else in the shade and absorb all nutrients and moisture from the soil. One or more of the existing trees will have to go, with the choice dictated by practical factors such as direction of light and proximity to the house as well as the gardener's personal likes and dislikes. Tree-felling and the proper refurbishment and maintenance of old neglected trees is specialized work for which professional help is essential.

The small selection of trees described in this chapter have been chosen for their decorative qualities. Most of them make ideal specimen trees – that is, they merit being planted in a spot where they attract attention, for example in the middle of a lawn. When choosing where to plant a young tree, consider first its place in the overall design of your garden, taking into account its ultimate size. Even small trees are much bigger than the shrubs, perennials, bulbs and bedding plants that grow around it; simply by virtue of its size, a tree draws the eye. You can use this quality to emphasize a line of perspective or to distract from a less interesting or frankly ugly view, as long as a nice balance is struck between trees and other plants. The time at which a tree is at its best is important here. If there is a corner of the garden dependent for spring colour on bulbs, but comparatively dull in the autumn, incorporate a tree which blazes with autumn colour, such as a witch hazel (*Hamamelis mollis*). If you find the blossom of the flowering cherry irresistible, site the tree where it will have no rivals in spring, but where its fading blossom will be compensated for by a swathe of summer colour from the border.

An equally important consideration when deciding where to plant a tree is that in a competition for light and nourishment from the soil, mature trees will always win. Do not plant them too close to other plants which will suffer. Dappled shade from a nearby tree is ideal for some plants, and very pleasant for human beings on a hot summer's day; but a large tree too close to the house can make the rooms dark (and the roots may damage the foundations, necessitating costly repairs).

There are several factors influencing the choice of ornamental trees. Evergreens are prized for year-round interest and, if planted together, for the protection from wind they provide. Deciduous trees may have attractively shaped leaves which change colour in the autumn or pretty blossom and showy berries. The shape of the tree itself is important too. Where space is limited columnar or upright trees are useful, like eucryphias and spruces. In a formal garden a compact, neat outline looks best, as with a sorbus, while spreading trees like laburnums suit informal settings. The importance of a deciduous tree's skeleton – what it will look like in winter with bare branches – is related to some extent to the situation. If the tree is in a very prominent position it is as well to ensure that it bears scrutiny even without its leaves.

PLANTING A TREE Even though 3-4-year-old trees ready for planting are relatively small, they are large enough to merit two pairs of hands when planting. The best time to plant is between autumn and spring for deciduous trees, in autumn or spring for evergreens. Do not attempt to work on soil that is frozen hard or waterlogged. Young trees may have their roots covered in a ball of soil and wrapped in polythene; they may be bare-rooted or in a container. Container-grown trees can be planted at any time, even in summer as long as the soil is never allowed to dry out. Inspect bare-rooted trees before planting, cutting back any dead or diseased roots to healthy tissue.

1 Make a planting hole 45cm/18in deep and 90cm/3ft in diameter. If planting on grass, remove the turves from a neat circle and set them aside.

2 Fork up the soil at the bottom to aerate it and aid drainage.

3 Put a solid wooden stake, treated with preservative, in the middle of the hole, knocking it in with a mallet. Place it so that the top will be just below the point where the tree starts to branch.

4 If the soil is wet and heavy, place a layer of drainage material 15cm/6in deep evenly over the bottom of the hole.

5 Chop up the reserved turves, if any, into small pieces and place them in the hole grass side down.

6 Fork in a 15cm/6in layer of well-rotted manure or organic compost and replace the soil to the half-way point. Tread it down.

7 This is where you need a second pair of hands. Person

A holds the tree in place in the hole, gripping low on the stem, while Person B rests a flat piece of wood across the hole. Line up the tree so that the old planting mark on the stem is level with the wood. It may be necessary to add or remove soil beneath the tree to get it to the right depth.

8 With the tree held upright against the stake, gradually replace the remaining soil in the hole. Give the tree a shake from time to time to help the soil settle.

9 When the roots are covered, strew 2 cupfuls of sterilized bonemeal over the rooting area and cover with 3-4 shovelfuls of peat.

10 Continue filling up the hole with soil, treading it down occasionally, until the old planting mark is just visible and the soil level.

11 Attach the tree to the stake with a strap, placing a rubber buffer between stem and stake. As the tree grows, the strap will need to be loosened accordingly.

CARE OF TREES Give young trees a moisture-retentive mulch every autumn or spring. Suitable materials are well-rotted compost, leaf-mould or peat, applied over the rooting area to a depth of 10cm/4in. Young trees need generous watering, especially in dry spells and if the soil is light in texture. Feeding is not usually necessary because the mixture in the planting hole releases its nutrients over a long period of time.

Mature trees do not normally need watering. They may, however, need feeding. Signs of undernourishment are discoloured or undersized leaves, or premature leaf fall. Apply a general fertilizer in granular form to the roots. Bore 30cm/12in deep holes in the soil at 60cm/24in intervals. Pour the granules into the holes through a funnel to within 4cm/1½in of the surface and top up with soil.

PROPAGATION Although the method of propagation suitable for specific trees is described in the individual entries that follow, in many cases raising trees is a lengthy and skilled process beyond the scope of most amateurs. Grafting is a particularly demanding technique used for many species. A scion or shoot from the tree you wish to propagate is joined to a suitable rootstock by one of several methods. In approach grafting, for example, a shallow slice of wood is taken from both the scion and the rootstock and the two wounds are bound tightly together until they unite, which usually takes about 3 months. At this point the top of the rootstock and the bottom of the scion are cut away. Different methods are appropriate to different species.

MAGNOLIA

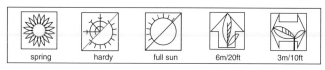

| spring | hardy | full sun | 6m/20ft | 3m/10ft |

Magnolias are among the most popular trees grown as specimens in a lawn or at the front of a town house. They bear huge, cup-shaped flowers of pink or white in early spring, often when it seems too cold for such beautiful blooms to survive – but they do, as long as they are sheltered from chilling winds.

GROWING Plant in spring in fertile, well-drained soil. Support with double stakes until well established. Top dress annually in spring with a 5cm/2in layer of well-rotted compost, peat or leafmould. No pruning is necessary.

PROPAGATION Take 10cm/4in cuttings of semi-hardwood shoots in summer and place in coarse sand in a propagating frame at 21°C/70°F. When rooted, pot on and overwinter in a cold frame. In spring, transfer to a nursery bed. Grow on for 3 years before transferring to permanent positions. Alternatively, layer suitable stems in spring (*see page 17*).

SPECIES *Magnolia salicifolia*, upright and fast-growing, star-shaped white flowers 10cm/4in wide open before the leaves unfurl. As the name indicates, the leaves are willow-like; *M. denudata*, up to 4.5m/15ft, slow-growing, abundance of fragrant white flowers 15cm/6in across.

POSSIBLE PROBLEMS Frost damage, grey mould, honey fungus.

▦ PLANTING TIP

When planting a new tree that needs staking, make sure the stake is placed in the hole with the roots before filling in to avoid damage to the root system.

LABURNUM

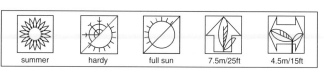

| summer | hardy | full sun | 7.5m/25ft | 4.5m/15ft |

Commonly known as golden rain, a laburnum tree in flower is a splendid sight. In late spring or early summer the branches are hung with long racemes of bright yellow flowers. All parts of the tree are highly poisonous, particularly the young green seedpods, which look like peas.

GROWING Plant between autumn and spring in any type of well-drained garden soil. A sunny site is best but semi-shade is tolerated. Provide stakes until the tree is established. No pruning is necessary.

PROPAGATION Species may be raised from seed sown in autumn in pots and set in a cold frame. Prick off the seedlings into boxes when they are large enough to handle. Transfer to nursery rows in spring and to the permanent site in the autumn. Hybrids and named varieties are propagated by grafting (*see page 119*).

SPECIES *L. alpinum* (Scotch laburnum), spreading habit, handsome bark in maturity, flowers in 25cm/10in racemes; 'Pyramidalis' is an erect form; *L. anagyroides* (common laburnum), 3m/10ft high, sometimes more, an early-flowering species with racemes 15-25cm/6-10in long. Named varieties include 'Pendulum', with a weeping habit, good for small gardens. *L. × watereri* (*above*), hybrid of moderate height. The variety 'Vossii' bears abundant, very long flower racemes.

POSSIBLE PROBLEMS Honey fungus, leaf miners.

▦ PLANTING TIP

Light and graceful, the laburnum is often chosen to be the focal point in a garden: it has the added advantage of casting dappled shade in which *other plants can grow. The most spectacular variety is L. × watereri 'Vossii', which has very long tassels of flowers – up to 50cm/20in long.*

SORBUS

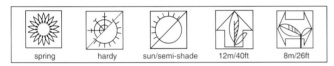

spring	hardy	sun/semi-shade	12m/40ft	8m/26ft

The genus *Sorbus* includes rowans, which are discussed here, and whitebeams. Rowans or mountain ashes are elegant trees admired for their pinnate leaves, which take on brilliant autumn tints. Flattened heads of tiny cream flowers appear in late spring, followed by attractive clusters of small round fruits.

GROWING Plant trees between autumn and spring in any type of well-drained soil in sun or semi-shade. Rowans tolerate the polluted atmosphere of towns well. No pruning is required.

PROPAGATION Pick the berries in autumn and take out the seeds. Sow immediately in seed compost in a cold frame. Prick the seedlings into boxes as soon as they are large enough to handle. Transfer to nursery rows in the following autumn to grow on for 5 years before planting in the final position.

SPECIES *S. hupehensis* (*above*), foliage blue-green, turning red in autumn, pale pink berries appear in late summer and last for weeks. *S. sargentiana*, height and spread 8m/26ft, leaves and fruit orange-red in autumn, best choice for colour; *S. vilmorinii*, height and spread up to 6m/20ft, dainty tree with fern-like leaves turning red in autumn, fruits red or white flushed pink.

POSSIBLE PROBLEMS Apple canker, fire blight, honey fungus.

PRUNUS

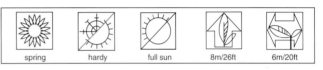

spring	hardy	full sun	8m/26ft	6m/20ft

The genus *Prunus* includes a huge number of trees that provide spectacular displays of spring flowers. Those described here are ornamental cherries; others are ornamental almonds, peaches, plums and cherry laurel. Easy to grow, all are popular in town gardens. Ornamental cherries have pointed, oval leaves and bear their blossom in heavy clusters.

GROWING Plant in autumn, not too deep in any well-drained soil, preferably with a little lime. Staking will be necessary until the tree is established, especially in exposed positions. Try not to disturb the soil around the trees too much, as they are shallow-rooting. No regular pruning is required. If necessary, damaged branches can be removed in late summer.

PROPAGATION By budding (*see page 18*) on to the rootstock *Prunus avium* (wild cherry).

SPECIES *P.* 'Amanogawa', upright habit, spread only 1.8-2.4m/6-8ft, good for small gardens, deep pink blossom; *P.* × 'Halle Jolivette', hybrid, height and spread 4.5m/15ft, suitable for small gardens, long-lasting double white flowers; *P.* 'Tai-Haku' (great white cherry, *above*), foliage red when young, bright white flowers 5cm/2in across, a vigorous grower.

POSSIBLE PROBLEMS Birds eat buds, caterpillars eat leaves; bacterial canker, chlorosis, honey fungus.

▓ ORGANIC TIP

A good choice if you are hoping to attract wildlife. The bright red berries look attractive and are a good source of food for birds in the autumn.

▓ ORGANIC TIP

This tree produces spectacular displays of flowers in spring, which are very attractive to insects and bees. Some varieties, such as *the ornamental cherry, are sterile but others produce small fruits which will attract birds into the garden in search of food.*

ROBINIA

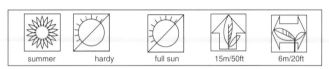

summer	hardy	full sun	15m/50ft	6m/20ft

The yellow-green, elegant foliage of *Robinia pseudoacacia* is best appreciated in larger gardens. Related to the laburnum (both are members of the pea family), robinias bear similar flowers in racemes up to 15cm/6in long in late spring or early summer. Short spines protrude along the stems.

GROWING Plant between autumn and spring in any type of well-drained soil in a sunny position sheltered from cold winds. Robinias tolerate atmospheric pollution and do well in areas of low rainfall; in waterlogged soils they are more vulnerable to wind damage. No pruning is required.

PROPAGATION Sow seed in pans of compost in early spring in a cold frame. Prick off into boxes when large enough to handle. Transfer to nursery beds and grow on for 3 years before planting in the permanent positions.

VARIETIES 'Frisia' (*above*), foliage opens bright yellow, turning light green in summer; 'Inermis' (mop-head acacia), compact, round habit, spineless branches, very few flowers.

POSSIBLE PROBLEMS Generally trouble-free.

SALIX

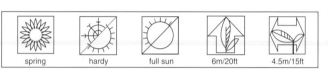

spring	hardy	full sun	6m/20ft	4.5m/15ft

Even if they cannot put a name to any other tree, most people can recognize a willow by its slender, pointed leaves and the woolly catkins which appear in spring. Some species also have colourful bark. All like moisture, and are often planted near water.

GROWING Plant between autumn and early spring in a sunny position. Light, sandy soils are unsuitable, especially for the larger species. To prune, remove dead wood during the winter and to encourage coloured shoots cut back to within 1-2 buds of old wood just before budbreak in spring.

PROPAGATION Take hardwood cuttings between autumn and spring and insert in moist soil. They should be ready for planting out in permanent positions after 1 year.

SPECIES *Salix daphnoides* (violet willow, fast-growing, with yellow catkins in early spring before the gleaming green leaves; in winter the stems are purple; *S. alba* (white willow), height up to 12m/40ft, greeny yellow catkins and grey-green leaves in late spring. *S. matsudana* 'Tortuosa' (*above*), slow-growing, erect willow. The variety 'Chermesina' has orange shoots in winter.

POSSIBLE PROBLEMS Caterpillars; anthracnose of willow.

▓ PLANTING TIP

Always take into account final size and shape when choosing a tree. This one grows tall; the variety 'Pyramidalis' is slender, forming a neat column.

▓ ORGANIC TIP

Ideal for the organic gardener, as the yellow woolly catkins not only look very attractive, but also provide food for early butterflies, moths and other insects.

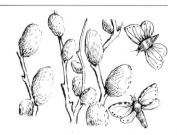

SAMBUCUS

| spring | hardy | semi-shade | 2.4m/8ft | 2.4m/8ft |

The common elder, *Sambucus nigra*, which reaches 4.5m/15ft in height, is a familiar sight in the wild with its flattened heads of creamy flowers and the clusters of purplish black berries that follow. *S. racemosa*, the red-berried elder, is a slower growing cousin which makes a handsome addition to the garden.

GROWING Plant between autumn and spring in any type of fertile soil, in partial shade. Prune to encourage colourful foliage by cutting the stems right back in frost-free weather between autumn and spring: this will, however, reduce the quantity of flowers and berries.

PROPAGATION Take 25cm/10in hardwood cuttings in late autumn and treat as for salix (*see page 122*).

VARIETIES *S. nigra*: 'Aurea', yellow leaves; 'Aurea-variegata', green leaves edged yellow. *S. racemosa*: 'Plumosa Aurea' (*above*), finely cut yellow leaves.

POSSIBLE PROBLEMS Aphids; arabis mosaic virus.

RHUS

| summer | hardy | full sun | 4.5m/15ft | 5m/16ft |

The stag's horn sumach, *Rhus typhina*, is chiefly grown for its stunning autumn foliage, though it bears dense, 20cm/8in long panicles of minuscule flowers in summer. These are followed by clusters of red berries. Take care when pruning, as the sap contains a substance which irritates the skin.

GROWING Plant between autumn and spring in ordinary soil. This species thrives even in polluted urban atmospheres. To prune, cut stems right back to ground level in early spring. This will encourage foliage at the expense of flowers and fruit.

PROPAGATION This species produces numerous suckers, which may be pulled off in the autumn and planted where they are to grow. Alternatively, suitable shoots may be layered in spring (*see page 17*). They should be ready to sever from the parent plant in 1-2 years.

VARIETIES 'Laciniata' (*above*), fern-like green leaves turn orange and yellow in autumn.

POSSIBLE PROBLEMS Poor growing conditions may cause die-back.

■ ORGANIC TIP

The sweet-smelling flowers of the elder attract bees and other insects into the garden – and they also make excellent wine. They are followed by red berries which are highly attractive to birds as a good source. The black berries of the common elder are also good for winemaking.

■ PLANTING TIP

The stag's horn variety, the most popular, is extremely prolific: prune regularly or it will become too leggy and bare. It is unsuitable for planting in lawns because of the numerous suckers it produces, which can soon take over if not destroyed quickly.

EUCRYPHIA

summer	hardy	sun/semi-shade	6m/20ft	1.8-2.4m/6-8ft

If you can offer a sheltered, position, perhaps with the protection of a warm wall, *Eucyrphia × nymansensis* would be a worthy candidate for the spot. Not fully hardy, in a favourable position it produces exquisite white, saucer-shaped flowers with a boss of red-tipped yellow stamens in late summer. These blooms are well set off by glossy oval leaves.

GROWING Plant in autumn on light soil, neutral or slightly acid. Eucryphias like sun or partial shade with a cool root run. In winter, protect young plants from frost with a covering of straw. Pruning is not necessary, but pinch out the leading shoots of young plants to encourage a bushy habit.

PROPAGATION Take 10cm/4in cuttings of non-flowering side shoots in late summer and insert in a peat/sand mixture at 16°C/61°F in a propagator. Pot up when rooted and overwinter in a cold frame. Harden off in the summer, keep sheltered over winter and plant out in the following spring.

VARIETIES 'Nymansay' (*above*), vigorous, upright habit, profusion of 7.5cm/3in wide white flowers in late summer.

POSSIBLE PROBLEMS Generally trouble-free.

PICEA

non-flowering	hardy	full sun	7.5m/25ft	2.5m/8ft

In natural conditions the Colorado spruce, *Picea pungens*, reaches 30cm/100ft, but numerous smaller forms of this beautiful tree have been raised for garden cultivation. Generally conical in shape, the trees bear stiff needles that are very pale blue-grey when young. After about 20 years cylindrical cones 7.5cm/3in long are produced.

GROWING Plant from autumn to spring on deep, moisture-retentive, slightly acid soil. Choose a sheltered position as young trees are vulnerable to damage by frost. Sprinkle a general-purpose fertilizer around the rooting area each spring. Pruning is not necessary.

PROPAGATION Sow seed in spring in boxes of compost in a cold frame. Place in nursery rows the following spring and grow on for 2-3 years before transferring to permanent positions.

VARIETIES 'Glauca', beautiful blue-green needles; 'Glauca Pendula', only 3 × 3m/10 × 10ft, a weeping form; 'Argentea', silver needles; 'Viridis', light green.

POSSIBLE PROBLEMS Green spruce aphids.

■ PLANTING TIP

If the tree looks pot-bound when planting, the roots should be gently teased out and spread out flat around the new hole. Make sure the hole is big enough.

■ PLANTING TIP

The silvery blue foliage of spruce is very attractive, so this tree is often used in gardens to provide a focal point. Remember always to keep in mind the final size of a tree when planting. After 10 years this tree will be approximately 2-3m/6-10ft tall but in time can reach 7.5m/25ft.

AMELANCHIER

spring	hardy	full sun	7.5m/25ft	4.5m/15 ft

Amelanchiers are very hardy trees, easily grown and as beautiful as their common name, snowy mespilus. Not only do they bear spectacular spring flowers, followed by round, edible fruits, but the autumn colour of the attractive oval leaves is exceptionally vivid.

GROWING Plant from autumn to spring in any type of moisture-retentive soil. A position in partial shade is tolerated. No pruning is required.

PROPAGATION Sow seed in summer in pots of compost in a cold frame. Transfer to a nursery bed when large enough to handle. Grow on for 2-3 years before planting in permanent positions. Alternatively, layer suitable branches in early autumn (*see page 17*).

SPECIES *A.* × *grandiflora* syn *A.* × *lamarckii* (*above*), hybrid between *A. canadensis*, whose woolly leaves turn yellow in autumn, and *A. laevis*, coloured red in autumn; leaves purple, downy when young, beautiful red in autumn; large racemes of white flowers. A pink-flowered form, *A.* × *grandiflora rubescens*, is also available.

POSSIBLE PROBLEMS Fireblight.

PYRUS

spring	hardy	full sun	7.5m/25ft	6m/20ft

The pear family does not include ornamental species to compare with the cherry in terms of showy flower-bearing. The beauty of *Pyrus salicifolia*, the willow-leaved pear, lies in its delicacy and grace. The narrow leaves, covered in silky white down, open in spring at the same time as the pure white flowers, closely packed in rounded clusters. As the leaves mature the down disappears, leaving them smooth and pale. The fruits are not edible.

GROWING Plant between autumn and spring in well-drained but moisture-retentive soil, avoiding open situations if possible. Water well until established. Do not dig around the roots – suppress weeds if necessary with a mulch of well-rotted compost or leaf-mould. No pruning is necessary except to remove crossing branches of established trees.

PROPAGATION Pears are increased vegetatively by grafting on to the rootstock of *Pyrus communis* (wild pear).

VARIETIES 'Pendula' (*above*), with drooping branches, reaches 5m/16ft and is a good choice for small gardens.

POSSIBLE PROBLEMS Woolly aphids, scale insects; fireblight.

■ PLANTING TIP

A spectacular-looking tree which will certainly brighten up a dark corner. But remember that this is a tree for the larger garden, as it will reach 4m/14ft or more in time. There is no need to prune, but cut back in winter, if necessary, to keep its growth in check.

■ PLANTING TIP

This graceful, elegant tree, which has great architectural merit, is ideal if you need a small ornamental tree to provide a focal point of interest in your garden.

HAMAMELIS

| winter | hardy | full sun | 2.4m/8ft | 2.4m/8ft |

Like the winter-flowering jasmine, witch hazels produce yellow flowers on bare stems before the leaves unfurl. They make good specimen trees or can be incorporated in a shrub border. The branches, with their spidery flowers, can be cut for decoration – they last well in water. In autumn the leaves take on beautiful coloured tints.

GROWING Plant between autumn and spring in slightly acid, moisture-retentive soil on a site sheltered from cold winds. Prune established specimens after flowering, cutting back unruly branches.

PROPAGATION Layer suitable shoots in early autumn (see page 17). Named varieties must be grafted on to rootstock of *Hamamelis virginiana* (common witch hazel) under glass.

SPECIES *H. × intermedia*, yellow flowers with crimped petals in very early spring, oval green leaves turn gold in autumn. Leaves of the named variety 'Hiltingbury' turn variously yellow, copper, scarlet and red in autumn – an outstanding choice. *H. mollis* (Chinese witch hazel, *above*), heavily fragrant yellow flowers flushed red appear in mid winter. Good, free-flowering forms are 'Brevipetala', with smaller blooms and 'Pallida', with paler petals.

POSSIBLE PROBLEMS Generally trouble-free.

ACER

| spring | hardy | semi-shade | 5.5m/18ft | 3m/10ft |

The maple family includes a large number of extremely handsome trees and shrubs, all bearing the characteristic palmate leaves which often take on vivid colours in autumn. The slow-growing *Acer palmatum* (Japanese maple) is a good choice for medium to small gardens. From this species a number of highly ornamental forms have been developed.

GROWING Plant from autumn to spring in well-drained, cool, moisture-retentive soil. Some lime is tolerated. Choose a site sheltered from sharp winds and early morning sun after frost. No pruning is required.

PROPAGATION The species may be raised from seed sown in the open in the autumn. Named varieties must be grafted on to species rootstock.

VARIETIES 'Atropurpureum' (*above*), bronze foliage; 'Dissectum', dwarf form with deeply cut leaves; 'Koreanum', striped bark, leaves brilliant red in autumn; 'Sessifolium Osakazuki' has the finest autumn colours – a combination of fiery orange, crimson and scarlet.

POSSIBLE PROBLEMS Aphids, red spider mites if conditions are too warm and dry; coral spot, honey fungus.

▓ CUT FLOWER TIP

A few branches with their delicate yellow flowers will provide a welcome touch of indoor colour when not much else is available. They also provide a lovely scent.

▓ PLANTING TIP

The beauty of this tree is that there are varieties available suitable for both small and large gardens. One particular variety, 'Atro-purpureum', is especially good for small gardens or patios, as it is only 60-90cm/2-3ft high and is highly ornamental, with purple leaves.

GLOSSARY

Acid Used to describe soil with a pH reading below 7.0. Because acid soils contain little lime, lime-hating plants like rhododendrons thrive in them.

Aeration Loosening of the soil to admit air.

Alkaline Used to describe soil with a pH reading above 7.0. A slightly alkaline soil suits most plants.

Annual A plant that completes its life cycle in one growing season.

Aquatic A plant that lives in water, sometimes with leaves and flowers floating on the surface.

Axil The angle between the stem and a leaf, from which further growth arises.

Bedding plant A plant used for temporary garden display.

Biennial A plant that needs two growing seasons to complete its life cycle.

Bract A modified leaf, which may be coloured and have the appearance of a petal.

Bulbil A small bulb that forms at the base of mature bulbs and which can be detached and grown on to achieve maturity.

Catkin A flower spike composed of bracts.

Chlorosis Deficiency of minerals in the soil giving a pale appearance to foliage.

Cloche Glass or plastic covering to protect plants in the open.

Compost 1 a mixture of loam, sand, peat and leaf-mould used for growing plants in containers. **2** rotted remains of plant and other organic material.

Conifer Trees and shrubs with needle-like leaves which bear their seeds in cones.

Corona From the Latin meaning a crown. Used to describe the trumpet of a narcissus.

Crown The bottom of a perennial such as lupin from which roots and shoots arise.

Dead-heading The practice of removing faded flowerheads in order to prevent seeding, encourage further flowering or to keep a plant looking tidy.

Dormant Literally, sleeping. Used to describe the period when a plant makes no growth, usually in the winter.

Evergreen A plant which bears foliage throughout the year.

Fungicide A substance used to combat fungal diseases.

Germination The first stage in the development of a plant from a seed.

Ground cover Plants used to cover the soil, smothering weeds with attractive foliage.

Half-hardy Used to describe plants that require protection during the winter.

Hardy Description of plants that survive frost in the open.

Hip Fruit of the rose.

Humus The substance remaining when dead vegetable matter has broken down.

Insecticide A substance used for killing insects.

Larva The immature stage of some insects, such as caterpillars and grubs.

Lateral A stem or shoot that branches out from the leaf axil of a larger stem.

Leader The main stem of a tree that extends the system of branches.

Lime Calcium, a chemical that may be used to neutralize acid soils. Too much lime makes it impossible for some nutrients in the soil to be absorbed by plants.

Loam Soil which is a compound of clay, silt, sand and humus. It is moisture-retentive and mineral-rich.

Mulch A layer of organic matter spread on the soil surface to conserve moisture.

Naturalizing The practice of growing plants in conditions that simulate nature.

Neutral Used to describe soil with a pH reading between 6.5 and 7.0, which is neither acid nor alkaline.

Node A joint in a plant's stem from which leaves, buds and side-shoots arise.

Offset A young plant that is naturally produced by mature plants and can be detached and used for propagation.

Organic Used to describe substances that are the product of the decay of living organisms.

Peat Partially decayed organic matter. Sedge peat is from the roots of sedges growing in bogs.

Perennial A plant that lives for an indefinite period.

pH reading The pH scale is used to measure the acidity or alkalinity of soil. The neutral point is 7.0; a reading above this denotes alkalinity and one below it denotes acidity.

Pinching out Removing the growing point of a stem to encourage bushy growth.

Pricking out Planting out seedlings for the first time to larger trays or to a nursery bed.

Propagation Increasing plants.

Pruning Cutting back a plant to keep the shape neat, restrict the size and encourage the formation of flowers.

Root run The soil area occupied by the roots of a plant.

Rootstock The name for the plant on to which another is grafted.

Scion A shoot of a plant joined to the rootstock of another. Used to propagate trees.

Seedling A young plant.

Spit A spade's depth - about 25-30cm/10-12in.

Stake A support for plants, from a cane for delphiniums to a heavy wooden stake for a young tree.

Stamen The male reproductive organ of a flower, arising from the centre of the petals.

Sucker A shoot that arises from below ground level. Suckers should always be pulled clean off, not cut.

Tender Used to describe any plant susceptible to damage by frost.

Tendril A kind of leaf or stem that twines around supports, permitting plants to climb.

Tilth The surface layer of the soil, which is fine and crumbly.

Transplanting Moving young plants from one place to another to give them more room to develop.

Vegetative Propagation by a part of the plant, i.e. offsets, cuttings, division of roots, layering of a stem, rather than by sowing seeds.

Whorl An arrangement of leaves or flowers that project from a single point like rays.

INDEX